Dedication and Thanks

I dedicate this book -

*To my parents; In a day where many couples separate, I thank
my parents for providing me the influence of both parents.
Most of what I learned in life is due to incredible parents, that
provided solid guidance, teaching and self-sacrifice for others.
My Dad taught me the importance of learning technical skills, as
well as educational knowledge. I have always been amazed by my
father and his amazing ability to do anything. I honestly believe
he has never faced a challenge he couldn't conquer. My mother
taught me to give of my time and effort to help others. She led by
example, volunteering to help others, but not for appreciation or
reward – simply for the ability that she had to help others in need.
Both showed exceptional examples of moral and ethical behavior.
While I can never repay them for all they have sacrificed for me
and my brothers, I want to thank them for everything that have
done for us.*

*To my wife; who has supported me unconditionally throughout
this project and everything in life. She allows me to keep things in
perspective and recognize what is truly important in life.*

Old School Business in the New Business World

Lessons learned by the Japanese, a brake throwing machine and a Pontiac truck

Ken Wright

Forward

First let me state this book does not reference ignoring new inventions, creations, ideas and technology, for which to stimulate our economic-growth. To the contrary, it focuses on basic business principles and methods for which to base decisions, utilizing innovation and technology within our new business culture. In addition to reading Chris Anderson's "Makers: the New Industrial Revolution", I was privileged to meet Mr. Anderson as well for a couple of days. While it was a rare opportunity that I was able to begin reading a book and continue reading until the last word, I found the author equally as intriguing as the book. While some interpreted Mr. Anderson's conversations as contrarian, it was more apparent to me that this was a man that simply questioned the logic and reason for using new technology. In certain areas of technology, we have solved the technology of capacity and bandwidth – however we have yet to create programs that would utilize these added resources in many cases. If his theory is correct that the future of manufacturing is headed toward a personal level and smaller manufacturers, how can we ensure these new entrepreneurs and small manufacturers have the basic business skills to effectively conduct a profitable and successful business?

I found common ground with Chris with regard to common sources that I have used in my manufacturing career. Chris referenced Mitch Free (whom I have also had the privilege to develop a friendship) in his book. Mitch Free is a serial entrepreneur and global leader best known for founding MFG.com, an online manufacturing marketplace named by the New York Times as one of 10 companies to change the world. In the beginning of MFG.com, I was amazed at the ease of use of a global sourcing web-based program. It truly allowed for submitting Requests for Quotations (RFQ's) globally, utilizing specific parameters and data related to the project, attaching of drawings in numerous formats and visual and data comparisons of detailed breakdowns for quotations. The robotics world is changing daily as evident by robots being programmed simply by showing them what to do. This elimination of programming skills provides the opportunity for individuals to utilize robotics technology without the expert programming skills of recent years. Albeit slow at this time, I suspect efficiencies of this robot will progress just as rapidly as other technologies have increased. This transformation that allows for individuals such as you and I to create and design products, globally source raw materials and implement robot-

ics technology to produce these goods - creates excitement for the po-

tential for economic growth for individuals. This same transformation

creates a sense of concern for these same individuals lacking the basic

business skills to effectively manage and grow their business.

CONTENTS

Have faith in your ideas!

More than twenty years ago as I began my manufacturing career with a Fortune 500 company, I was hired to learn all new equipment and processes at a start-up facility. Fresh from college and eager to learn, I immersed myself in the daily operations of the plant. My purpose was to become an expert on each piece of equipment with regard to setup and operation. This would subsequently allow me to train new employees as they were hired into the company. I was exposed to technology which I had not been previously exposed and relished the opportunities to learn from the equipment installers and maintenance technicians the purposes of each proximity switch, controller, relay and sensor. This stimulated my mind to think of future applications using these same technologies while allowing myself to be more creative in my own ideas. During one particular implementation of equipment, the engineer (Tim) assigned to the department approached me with a project. The basic concept of this project was to create a "universal" fixture for use in grinding, slotting and chamfering brake pads.

The reason was simple, save costs. The pieces of equipment that per-formed these operations included approximately 15 fixtures for which to place disc brake pads onto a conveyor. These fixtures were prohibitively expensive, as each was machined to replicate the exact bottom surface of the applicable brake pad. It was immediately visible that purchasing specific fixtures for each brake pad would not only be extremely expensive in fixture costs, but extensive changeover time would create inefficiencies and storage for each set of fixtures would create additional costs. My mission was to create a set of fixtures that could run as many different part numbers/brake pads as possible, without having to changeover the machine. The company had already obtained samples of every disc brake pad applicable to these machines, along with precise drawings for each applicable brake pad. Tim asked that I work on this project without sharing publicly my efforts and intent. What I did not realize at the time was that the same project was given to other engineers, so that they could achieve the same result.

Having no background in engineering, Catia or IGES drawings, blueprints, etc... I relied on the only method I knew to create a new fixture. I pulled every single part number from our sample inventory, placing each part on a rectangular piece of steel. My "high-tech" approach to marking the flanges, nibs and protrusions on the back of each brake pad was to place White-Out˚ on the protruding piece of the brake pad. This allowed for a clearly legible white dot to be placed on my steel plate at points of contact. I performed this same exercise over 200 times to specifically mark each plate.

This process took a few days to complete, but in reality all I needed for the final design was enough flat plate for which these brake pads could rest upon – to remain flat and stable for their intended operation (whether grinding, slotting or chamfering). With the dept engineer's permission, I enlisted the assistance of a technician (Todd) in the machine shop to train me in the use of a mill and lathe. It also allowed me to partner with this technician for his input into creating this "universal" fixture. Basically we removed the areas of the plate marked in white and confirmed the process by placing (you guessed it) each brake pad back into the fixture to ensure each pad would lie flat with no interference. What we found was that while the brake pads would lie flat, there was not a method to secure the pad onto the plate. At this point, our creativity expanded to use slides to lo-cate each part. Basically we milled slots through the plate and used round slides that could be loosened via Allen wrench and slid to close proximity of the brake pad. This would allow for the part to lie flat while at the same time prohibiting the part from shifting or sliding off the plate.

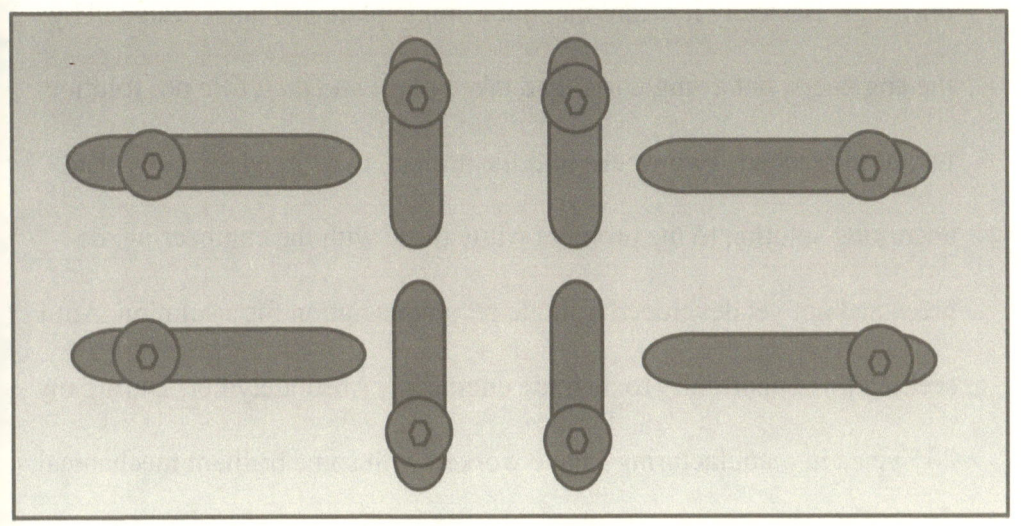

(Yes I created this drawing in Paint but you get the idea)

Upon completing the fixture, I performed trials on numerous brake pads to ensure that tolerances and dimensions related to thickness, degree of chamfer, thickness and placement of slots, etc... were all met in accordance with specifications. The "universal" fixture worked to perfection!

This process took a couple of weeks and I was afraid my boss's patience might be wearing thin. Todd and I called Tim down to the machine to show him the results of our efforts.

This is the moment we found out that other engineers were assigned to the project and were still trying to sort through all the drawings and overlay them to reverse engineer a fixture based upon a conglomeration of all the drawings. Basically it meant that not a single plate had been designed by the engineers, not a single trial had taken place and therefore no solution had been reached. Two weeks into the project, two "good ole boys" had a working solution to the problem while those with the engineering degrees had not yet developed a single recommendation for a solution. Am I seeking this opportunity to degrade engineers? Absolutely not! During my 20+ years in manufacturing I have worked with some brilliant mechanical, electrical, process, software, manufacturing, industrial and automotive engineers! I readily admit I pale in comparison to the majority of those that I have worked with during my career. However in this example the basic goal was being overshadowed by the engineers, while spending more time and resources determining how to "prepare" to reach the goal. Once again, tireless efforts toward "preparing" for the project or event does not translate into an effective project or event. We are all aware of the person that prepares the multiple page agenda and detailed outline of a project or an event. They work constantly at updating the agenda, notifying all participants, updating charts & graphs, relaying information via web updates, emails and phone calls – only to serve to update the agenda, not to complete the project or event. Once again, tireless efforts toward "preparing" for the project or event does not translate into an effective project or event.

Consult the experts - Operators

I have witnessed during a recent period of recession, numerous meetings detailing the planning of how to implement the most effective layoff system for employees. Numerous meetings were held at this company to discuss options, seniority, skills gaps, company needs, compensation, etc.... Please don't misunderstand me, because I am fully aware these are responsible considerations when this situation presents itself. However during this same period of time, I was able to locate numerous stamping, painting and welding jobs to eliminate the need to implement these planned layoffs. Don't get so caught up in your current mission that you forget your primary purpose for existence. The company had failed to realize if efforts had been directed to expand their customer base, layoffs could have been avoided completely. Many companies were hit hard during the recent recession, but companies that took advantage of opportunities to diversify their customer base and expand their products often came back stronger than before the recession. Permit me to relate a story of spending effort and time on research, planning and ideas – rather than simply consulting the expert: the operator. One of the pieces of equipment at the brake plant allowed for grinding of the disc brake pads on both sides of the pad. The ground pads discharged at the bottom of the machine, typically into a tote for future drilling. While the entry chute for stacking these brake pads allowed for the operator to "load" the machine chute at waist level, the discharge chute required that once the tote was full the operator would have to lift up the totes from floor level to place on a cart or carry to the next machine. Obviously the ergonomics of this operation could have led to discomfort at the least and injury at the worst. Therefore the challenge was issued to allow these ground brake pads to be conveyed back to waist level, thereby eliminating the need for the operator to bend over and lift product. Once again an engineering technician was given the assignment to eliminate this problem. He reviewed concepts of a chute/slide that would return the parts to waist-level, the smoothness of the surface needed to allow these brakes to slide on the chute, the material grade for which to make the chute, reviews of whether pneumatic or hydraulic cylinders would provide a better option for pushing these brake pads back to waist-level of the operator and even if the tubing of the pneumatic cylinder could withstand the dust associated with friction material.

The final concept was determined and the technician worked tirelessly to weld and form the stainless steel into shape, attaching the pneumatic cylinder, installing sensors to detect the presence of a brake pad that needed to be pushed forward and a counter to count the number of brake pads being produced. The end result looked something like a skeet throw.

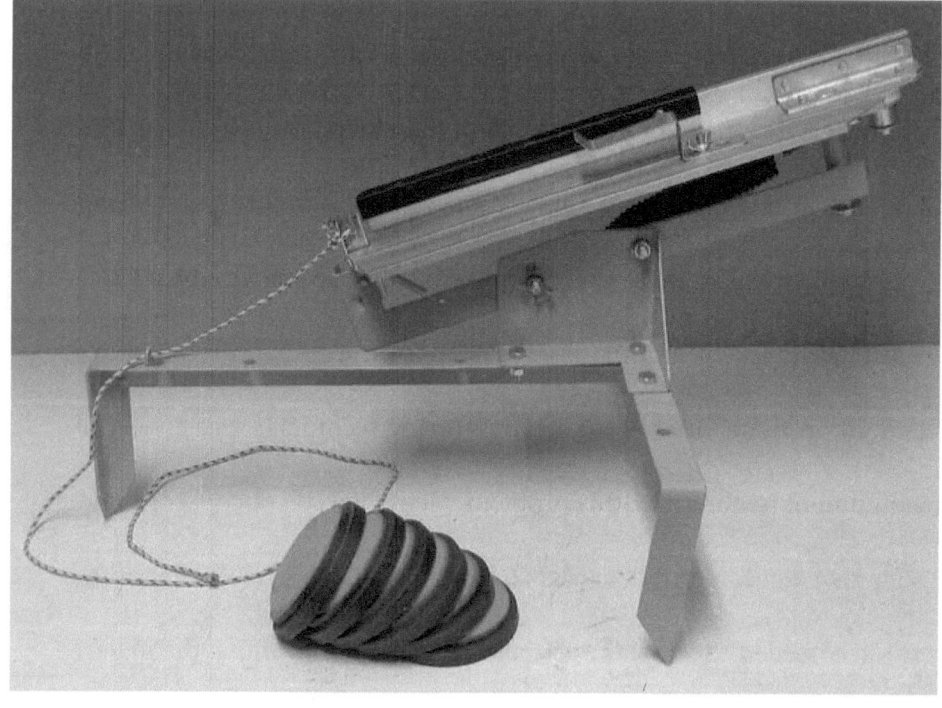

(Okay, so this isn't the real creation, but it actually looks amazingly similar!)

The engineering tech brought the "contraption" down to the machine. I inquired as to the purpose of this invention, but was told I would find out in just a few moments. When the technician returned with the engineering manager, it was then revealed to me the purpose of this "stacking" machine. During their discussion of describing how the machine addition would actually work, I briefly interrupted to state it would not work as described. While the technician took into account numerous factors related to making this machine addition work for long-term use, he simply forgot to take into account "gravity". While the brake pad was discharged from the bottom of the machine into the chute, the proximity sensor detected the presence of the pad and immediately activated the air cylinder to push the brake pad up the stainless steel chute. The brake pad glided effortlessly up the chute, but yes you guessed it – as soon as the cylinder retracted, the brake pad slide back up against the cylinder! The technician had not asked the operator for input, had not properly reviewed a "model" of the idea before proceeding and therefore the result was humiliation for the technician and wasted money for an ineffective solution. In the end, the need could have been met to satisfy the scope and purpose of the project - simply by installing a small belt conveyor.

A basic premise of improving an operator's efficiency or safety would be to consult the operator – right? The person that operates the equipment or machinery every day has the most intimate knowledge of its operation, safety concerns, needs for improvements, etc…. To be willing to humble yourself before others and ask their expertise

towards solutions not only avoids embarrassing situations like the ones

I mentioned prior, but also creates an atmosphere of working together

toward common goals. This basic understanding of doing business

is no less important than the basics of supply & demand, controlling

costs, controlling inventory, motivating your workforce, continuous

improvement, LEAN principles, etc....

Know your inventory

One of my managerial duties for an automotive-related manufacturer was to assimilate the weekly performance reports, denote performance to objectives and denote both areas of achievement and improvement. Within these measurable were competing metrics that allowed for a desire to have lower sales?! In addition, there was a great focus on removing and reducing line-side inventory along with a concern regarding inventory turns. Efforts were led to focus on specific areas and directed towards specific employees. What was missed during these efforts, was the business sense or logic towards just randomly reducing or increasing numbers and figures. So while one person was working to increase a metric, another was working toward another figure that would decrease the same metric. One person's efforts to remove the line-side inventory were being opposed by another person's efforts to eliminate multiple material handling by delivering directly to the point of use (line-side) from the receiving truck. After all, doesn't it make more sense to handle raw materials and components only once, rather than twice? Since the inventory had the same value on the line (before labor was added) as it did in the yard or in the warehouse, it actually wastes money to move the product more than once.

Subsequently there was a directive to increase inventory turns, which is typically a positive goal. Purchasing began implementing cuts to orders and minimizing quantities to have the "desired" effect to inventory turns, without realizing the added labor and hours to accommodate the additional shipments for every part number far exceeded the capacity of the receiving department. This "direction" of efforts from the top was killing this manufacturing plant. An equally important consideration is how focusing on inventory turns can negatively affect your profitability. Increases in freight costs, price increases from suppliers, handling costs and inventory processing costs are all possible risks to consider and are therefore primary considerations in the balance of managing inventory turns.

If you are paying the freight costs, then these costs will increase for more frequent deliveries. Simply put, if you can accommodate the receipt of one month's worth of material utilizing one truck, then that justifies a substantial savings over spreading this same amount of material over four weekly shipments per month.

A detailed cost analysis should be performed to determine if the costs savings for improving inventory turns exceeds these extra freight costs.

As a general rule of thumb, if the material costs are relatively low then it is not valid to focus on inventory turns for low-cost materials. Also important to consider (particularly in frequently changing markets such as steel/plastic/wire/electronics/food/chemicals) that price variations are common and there may be possible costs savings by purchasing these types of materials prior to price increases. Handling costs (both labor and inventory processing) will increase as inventory turns increase. This is an inevitable evil due to these repetitive functions being performed multiple times for multiple shipments instead of a single time for a single shipment. Once again, a cost analysis should be performed to account for both labor costs to handle material (unloading, receiving, locating in storage) along with the labor costs to perform data entry functions into your inventory management system.

In certain businesses there are also increased costs with regard to the accounts payable function. Many suppliers charge processing fees per invoice. On average an invoice cost $15 to $50 per invoice to process. Therefore if your business requires that you generate separate purchase orders and invoices for each specific shipment, this in turn will increase the costs to process these invoices for payment.

A greater issue was recognized with the "inventory inaccuracy" problem of the facility. During my recruitment to this company, I was informed of the ongoing concern for inventory inaccuracies. The facility would routinely run out of parts, due to the inability for tracking inventory. To magnify these discrepancies, this was a facility that allowed for substitutions to products of which many were not recorded. To add to these concerns, was a manual scrap recording system that did very little to resemble a system and even less to record scrap. However, upon reviewing the scrap and substitution issues there was still further issues to generate the inventory discrepancies I was reviewing. While the system was rather antiquated (AS400 MRP system), I honestly did not find the system to be of the primary concern. I continue to be a proponent that the best system in the world will fail with bad input and data entered into it. The main question remained, was accurate data being entered into the system? What I found with regard to their "supply chain" system was disturbing. The facility would receive shipments from one of the ancillary facilities two to three times per week on average. This would consist of materials produced at the other facility and demand calculated, based upon what was showing more than one week prior. The demand time fence created one set of problems, particularly for orders that were a rush order, not entered into the system correctly originally, orders affected by engineering changes, etc.... Unbelievably this was not remotely close to their most severe issue. What I found is that the multiple shipments were not received into the system (at our plant) until the FINAL shipment physically arrived. Paperwork for each truck did not exist with regard to having the ability to receive each truck individually into inventory. The multiple destructive effects of this cannot be over-emphasized. Parts were being used from the truck on Monday before the parts were even received into inventory into the system! Magnifying this issue was the random substituting of parts in production for which there was no ability at the end of the week (when the parts finally were received into the system) to determine which parts had been used. This also led to a morale problem due to the forceful approach being administered to one of the employees specifically designated to cycle counting! With the ever-present issues related to inventory discrepancies, the facility had assigned a full-time employee to the specific task of cycle counting raw materials and components every single day! I will run you through the example denoting the discrepancies created by this process – even if the part number was cycle counted DAILY:

Part A	Monday	Tuesday	Wednesday	Thursday	Friday
Beginning system inventory : Cycle count printed (a)	25	60	40	70	50
1st truck delivery @ 12 noon (b)	50	0	50	0	50
Qty used for daily production (c)	20	20	20	20	20
Received in system	0	0	0	0	150
Counted on cycle count @ 6 hrs of production (a+b- .75c); entered end of day in system	60	40	70	50	80
Actual inventory in location at end of day	55	35	65	45	75

Let's walk through one week of activity. On Monday, 25 pcs of Part A

was available in the system and in the physical location. For this example

we will assume inventory counts on Monday were correct in the system

and in the stock location. At noon, the first truck for the week delivering

this part would arrive, with the 50 pcs of product delivered by receiving

to the stock location. At the time the cycle counter arrived at the stock

location to count Part A, 15 pcs had been used for daily production. Please

be aware the cycle count sheet would reflect the 25 pcs on-hand at the time

of the printing of the cycle count sheet, however 60 pcs would be present

at the location at the time the counter performed his inventory check. The

cycle counter would enter quantities at the end of the day, after 5 more pcs

had been used for production. I know what you are thinking. What about the backflushing or issuing of components that occurs in the system with the recording of daily production? Well, cycle count data was entered as a fixed quantity – completely ignoring what quantities had been backflushed or issued to production. Basically this process was negating the important concept of automatic inventory removal, for those parts that appeared on the cycle count generation list.

Please note that because inventory was not maintained "real time", numerous errors were present in the cycle count process. Notice that the beginning inventory quantities for each day do NOT accurately depict the correct quantity for the part number. As cycle count sheets are printed for the quantity showing in the system at the beginning of the day, but yet physically counted 6 hours later – notice the disparity between actual inventory quantities and quantities entered into the system. Also please make note that the quantities counted during the cycle count process were not entered until two (2) hours AFTER the counts occurred. Basically our cycle counter would count material in the plant and adjust quantities in the system later than the counts, but days prior to the receiving process. Since inventory counted had not yet even been received into the system, the material was used during the week for production – at the end of the week the receiving paperwork would be entered into the system falsely denoting the quantity of these materials and components in inventory AFTER they had already been used!

The reality of the situation is that cycle counting the same part did NOT occur daily. Basically in the example above, the cycle count would review the quantities on Monday, enter the revised count at the end of the day and subsequent cycle count sheets would not denote this part number again for the week. How does that affect this scenario? Moving into the second day, the inventory quantity in the system would reflect a quantity of sixty (60) pcs. Sixty (60) pcs are backflushed Tuesday-Thursday (20+20+20) showing an inventory qty of ZERO (0) pcs in the system. This would generate a zero inventory report that denotes a parts emergency situation. The first step was to send the cycle counter to the location to confirm the inventory qty. Upon reaching the location, the counter would confirm the presence of forty-five (45) parts (55 end of day Monday – 20 used Tuesday + 50 received Wednesday – 20 used Wednesday – 20 used Thursday). The cycle counter would then enter this new qty of 45 pcs into the system, however not without the accusations of Purchasing and Production Control that he originally counted this part number incorrectly earlier in the week!

After all, how could you possibly count the quantity of a part earlier in the week, then be 45 pcs off 3 days later?! Please continue to understand that at the end of the day (Friday in this scenario) the system would reflect 175 pcs on-hand (45 on-hand Thursday – 20 pcs used Friday + 150 pcs received Friday); when in reality only 75 pcs would be available for production! Without the quick fix to correct the shipping and receiving system (shipping and receiving paperwork for each individual truck entered at the time of receipt), I immediately suspended the cycle counting process. While I fully recognize that is NOT the most effective corrective action nor the optimal solution, it was a required action at the time to stop perpetuating a known problem. While I won't elude to the inconsistent and errant methods of relieving inventory (backflush, issue, freestock) used for production as well, I will tell you that inventory began to stabilize to some measure. After choosing a clean breakpoint for which all shipments had been received and all materials/components had been backflushed or relieved from production, we began to run the facility with no cycle counts. Once again, I can't emphasize enough that I fully understand how inherently wrong it is to monitor inventory this way- or rather the failure to monitor inventory. So the process began; we had a beginning balance and I placed stricter controls on the reporting of substitutions and scrap. The trucks would come in during the week and parts would be used for production and we would not monitor the inventory level of any part in the plant during the week. At the end of the week after the last truck had been received and all inventory receipts for the week were entered into the system, I would perform some cycle counts myself to monitor effectiveness – but only after all transactions had been entered and inventory was stagnant.

Unfortunately this typically required weekend cycle counts. I found very little issues, with those being related to unreported substitutions and scrap. Parts outages decreased and with the exception of "freestock" parts, were practically eliminated. For those of you not familiar with the concept of freestock, I do not recommend it for an inventory control system. This new strange process of running the supply chain and inventory continued for months leading up to physical inventory. Unfortunately during this time, the corporate office was leaning on our Director to perform our cycle counts. While I explained the increased errors that would result if cycle counting resumed, it was not well-received by the Director and his corporate superiors. Luckily before cycle counts were to be resumed, a physical inventory was conducted. During the months of this change, continual training on inventory usage, substitutions, scrap reporting and production reported occurred with each department. I emphasized the critical importance of accurately reporting information to sustain production and eliminate downtime. The workforce stepped up to the task and at physical inventory the variance recognized was approximately $100. Yes I fully realize that even one part number could have skewed the amount more than $100, so there is a degree of luck within this result. However, this result was the smallest variance ever recognized at any of the multiple facilities within the company nationwide. The basic need was to "maintain" an accurate inventory level. Don't follow blindly to directions if you suspect the methods create failure. All businesses, industries and situations are not the same! This was an extremely abnormal process for me to intentionally recommend the cessation of a cycle counting process. I had always been a proponent of cycle counting inventory, but the situation dictates the process. In a typical manufacturing environment inventory adjustments are real-time, whether it be receipts, backflushing or issuing of materials or cycle count adjustments themselves. However if you aren't open to investigating all possibilities when researching problems, you may never find a solution. Don't assume!

To this point I have referenced trusting YOUR observations and inherent knowledge toward approaching problems. Directly communicate with the experts in the operation, meaning the persons that perform the operation on a daily basis. Don't spend so much time in the preparation and presentation of what you are planning to do, be more involved in the active role of accomplishing your goal! Don't get so caught up in "measurables" that you forget the most important measurable, to make profit! KNOW your inventory, even if it requires using unorthodox methods to do so! Many businesses and industries struggle with effective methods and procedures to maintain an accurate inventory. Consider the banking industry. Each day a bank knows their exact inventory, performs thousands of transactions each day and once again at the end of the day – knows their exact inventory. If banking is capable of maintaining a 100% accurate inventory every day, why then is it so difficult for manufacturing to accomplish this same goal?

Know your costs

There are many effective seminars and books regarding LEAN principles.

But what is the ultimate goal of LEAN? Is it not to reduce costs? Even

when coupled with the quality improvements LEAN can generate, the

net result is one of reduced costs. It is this area of reducing costs I would

like to review. Whether you are considering the tools of 5S, value stream

mapping, KANBAN, one piece flow, standardization of components, etc...

simply setup a model of your operation to determine which tools in the

toolbox apply to your organization and which tools would provide benefit.

Place a table in a room for each specific operation (receiving, stamping,

welding, machining, painting, assembly, shipping) and have specific items

assigned for each area of use. This exercise can be accomplished as simply

as the triangular wooden game with golf tees (like you find at Cracker

Barrel). We'll allow the stamping department to utilize the wooden

triangular bases, welding -blue golf tees, machining - green golf tees,

painting - red golf tees, assembly - yellow golf tees. As you would in your

manufacturing operation, employ a couple of material handlers to move

product from receiving to the departments and ultimately to shipping as

finished goods. Inform each department that they will request whatever product they want to operate their department efficiently and effectively. Begin with your materials "golf tees" in the warehouse, only accessible by the material handlers. Now is the time for the fun to begin….. as you start your stopwatch, listen for the immediate requests to your 2 material handlers from each of the departments – asking for materials. Some ask for 5, some ask for 10, etc…..material handlers realize that the stamping dept has to begin the process with the base so they deliver them first, subsequently they begin delivering to welding, machining, painting, assembly , etc.. Stamping performs their operation on their first 5-10 bases and requests a material handler to move the base to the next operation, subsequently welding works to complete these same 5-10 bases (inserting blue tees) at their operation and requests for the material handler to move to the next station. Granted during this time, both stamping and welding are requesting more materials so that they can continue to produce and be "efficient". Insert an operation to also "paint" the bases by coloring with a coloring pen or Sharpie. As this process progresses, notice when the first "finished good" arrives in shipping – call TIME. Make note of the time it required to produce ONE finished good and then do the following. Count the WIP (work in process) at each area of the process (stamping, welding, machining, painting) along with assigning some cost accounting to add labor costs into each area (additional $1 for each progression of stations). Now ask for input from the group, requesting areas for improvement (i.e. – do we need more material handlers, can we eliminate some of the material handling, can we perform some tasks off-line, can the supplier perform some of the operations and eliminate the need at our facility – such as painting the bases). Run through the example again? Is the operation faster? Do we need to practice "one piece flow"? Suggest as an option to line up the tables in order of process completion and instruct each participant that they are only allowed to handle ONE item at their station at a time, completing their current work before accepting the next item. Run the same scenario for the same amount of time as above (5-10 minutes or so). At the end of this time, check the following:

How many finished goods are in shipping?

How many items are in WIP at each station?

What is the value of the WIP in process?

Is there any change to morale (particularly with material handlers)?

Also, what is the value of storing your materials "golf tees" in the ware-house, rather than lineside? For raw materials, isn't the cost of the raw materials the same whether it is in a warehouse or lineside? Can there be cost savings recognized by the elimination of double-handling from the warehouse to the line and the associated labor costs to move these materials? What I expect you to realize is that by simply using common sense to eliminate extra material handling, arranging your plant flow in a logical order and completing one task at a time before proceeding to the next – you will find significant increases in efficiency, throughput and morale. At the same time you will notice decreased costs related to WIP and labor costs. In which scenario do you feel quality of production would be higher – attempting to produce in the first scenario or concentrating specifically on the one part in your area prior to working on the next? Basic management of your processes, your plant layout, your production method and inventory control are essential in sustaining profitability and growth. All operations are NOT the same, so don't try to apply a principle that has no place in your operation. For example, KANBAN is an effective method to manage inventory for certain applications. As Materials Manager for a Tier I automotive supplier, our company produced injection molded front and rear bumpers for multiple automotive models. The new plant was built with space allowed to store numerous pieces of each of these bumpers, so that inventory could be pulled upon demand from the customer – particularly for expedited replacement of a quality defect, for example.

Shelves were filled with level upon level of bumpers, each of which had to be identified and tracked. However, an associate had the brilliant idea to stop inventorying these bumpers in pallet racks and on shelves – but rather setup a KANBAN inventory of these bumpers in the production area itself. This required that six (6) different bumpers would require a storage area, only to contain the number of bumpers that could be run during the timing of a press changeover. Our company did have four (4) different presses, so it allowed for this process to work effectively. Basically a PULL system was initiated that worked backwards through our system – eventually requiring that the bumper we needed to paint from injection molding dept for a specific bumper was pulled from the KANBAN storage rack. This triggered the changeover of the applicable mold for that bumper so that production continued to run with product from the storage rack while the applicable mold was being installed into the press. Once the last bumper was pulled from the rack, the press was generating additional product from which to use for production. Production continued with product directly from the press, until no further product was needed from the press. The press continued to run until the KANBAN storage rack was refilled entirely. This same process was used for all six (6) variations of bumpers.

28

This allowed for an increase in storage rack space for external sourced materials, since this space was not being consumed by bumpers. It also allowed for a decrease in material handling of the additional bumpers. Furthermore, it provided less opportunity for damaged product – a HUGE unexpected benefit applicable to these OEM automotive bumpers. Obviously the KANBAN system provided great benefit to this operation. However, KANBAN's are clearly the wrong choice for other applications. Please don't make the mistake of using ideas and tools that are very effective for some uses, in areas for which they will provide no use or could provide harm. I recently heard Mitch Free make an extremely valid argument to avoid LEAN principles in creating your supply chain, as this can restrict competition in sourcing.Sure it is easy to apply some standard principles to your business (such as 5S), as these principles are easy to relate to most businesses and industries. Mapping out your processes to identify any areas for which the customer would not reward you financially, can typically provide value stream mapping benefits to any business.

The ethics of business

I would be remiss in speaking of the basics of business if I didn't include a brief discussion about the ethics of business. Sure everybody knows that you should give a full day's effort for a full day's pay, that you should report to work on-time and leave on-time, that you should never falsify documentation, that you should act professionally and dress appropriately. These are not specifically the types of ethics I would like to discuss, however as expressed to me almost weekly by manufacturers – these are issues that need to constantly be addressed. These "soft skills" appear to be lacking in our entry-level workforce. During my career I have had to make a few difficult decisions related to issues that I knew could affect my employment, but issues that created internal conflict regarding my own personal ethics and morals if I chose to ignore. For these types of reasons I also believe basic instincts kick in and people know if they are doing their jobs correctly, working professionally and truly earning the salary for which they are being paid. One of the most beneficial traits in your work ethic is trust, never allow that to be compromised.

Some view it unethical that a man capable of throwing a 95 mph fastball can earn millions of dollars per year, while a man can become an EMT and save lives and support his fellow man – but will fail to earn more than a few dollars per hour. For those that dedicate their lives to helping mankind (doctors, nurses, EMT's, police, fire, teachers, etc..), does it seem fair that those in professional sports earn salaries far in excess of those that truly affect human lives. That is not a slam against professional sports players, nor does it mean that many gifted athletes fail to affect human lives. There are numerous instances of athletes that support charities and individuals in need. These athletes use their wealth and position to establish and support those in need and for those I am humbled by their efforts. It is difficult to understand why we prioritize by wages those with athletic skills over those with teaching skills, healthcare skills or skills that are effective in creating economic growth. I agree these appear to be warped priorities, but not a matter of ethics.

I have signed agreements with corporations prohibiting the sharing of proprietary information or intellectual property. It is a shame that such agreements must exist, due to lack of ethics and morals in business. While I am concerned about the need for such agreements in our present day society, I also recognize that the smart businessman/businesswoman will realize the need for such agreements. Isn't it ironic that we have to sign written documentation to prohibit stealing from a company, sharing company information, using the internet inappropriately, etc....? Should not our inherent high standards of ethics prohibit should conduct? If you question internally whether your conduct and actions are appropriate in your business, chances are they are not. During my tenure as Purchasing Manager for a Tier I OEM automotive supplier, I received a quotation from a supplier reflecting pricing I knew to be incorrect. Based upon other suppliers quotations and my knowledge of materials cost, process cost, labor cost, packaging cost and freight cost – I knew the potential supplier had quoted a price that would result in a loss for their company. While I suspect some would take advantage of the "great deal" while it lasted, is this ethically the right thing to do? Certainly the quote was legal, signed by a company official and legally was a binding agreement. Shouldn't ethics require that the supplier be informed of the mistake and allowed to requote at a profit? Isn't the goal to form business "relationships" with your suppliers? I informed the supplier of the mistake and allowed them to resubmit the quotation – including the provisions and conditions which could negatively affect their quotation.

This same approach should be taken with your customers. A Tier I OEM automotive customer worked with me to determine build-out quantities for an upcoming model change. Basically this process consists of reviewing the intended number of vehicles to be produced through its current year model and subsequently determine the materials and components needed to build this number of vehicles. Additional parts remaining after the final vehicle is produced are many times obsolete and written off as scrap. For some parts, an allowable amount of "service parts" inventory is acceptable. The Production Control specialist would review these same build-out requirements with domestic, international and internally supplied materials and components. Based upon the EDI forecast, I noticed a discrepancy between the number of vehicles to be produced and the number of parts forecasted to supply. Upon reviewing in detail it was revealed we were correct in our assessment of the quantity of parts that we should supply, rather than the quantity our OEM customer was asking us to supply. Once again, we had a forecast and orders to justify shipping these excess quantities, which would have allowed us to be paid for these components. However, is this an ethical approach to generate more sales? The OEM's Production Control specialist met at our facility, during which we spent a few hours running through all the numbers. The net result – our customer reduced their international orders, orders from internal suppliers and issue revised build-out numbers to domestic suppliers. This adjustment saved our customer millions of dollars in obsolescence and created a strong, trusting relationship with our company.

Government's effect to your business

Don't be misled into thinking that you can focus on your business and ignore governmental affairs. Those that start a business or manage a business, whether small business or large industry, need to realize quickly that governmental affairs have an important impact on your success! Pericles quoted in 430 B.C. – "Just because you do not take an interest in politics doesn't mean politics won't take an interest in you!"

Whether the implications of stricter emissions regulations for manufacturing or increasing minimum wage for small business or the implementation of the Affordable Care Act which basically impacts both large and small business and practically every citizen – the need to educate yourself to the implications of governmental regulations is of primary concern. Ironic is the word "affordable" in the Affordable Care Act. It reminds me of the saying by P.J. O'Rourke "If you think healthcare is expensive now, wait until you see what it costs when it's free!" For each of these issues and others, I sincerely hope that our legislators run these scenarios through the same modeling process that I recommend for business decisions.

Take for example the soot emissions regulations being handed down to industries. First, please let me emphasize I am not opposed to emissions regulations. I do believe it is our responsibility to provide clean air and water for our citizens and future generations. What I question is the degree to which America should provide such greater and limiting restrictions to our emissions while recognizing that air is not stagnant – meaning the air over America doesn't simply hover over America. While legislation has been presented in America to reduce soot emissions from .75 ppb (parts per billion) down to .25 ppb, in China the average soot emissions levels are 3.5 ppb and in some cities 5 ppb!

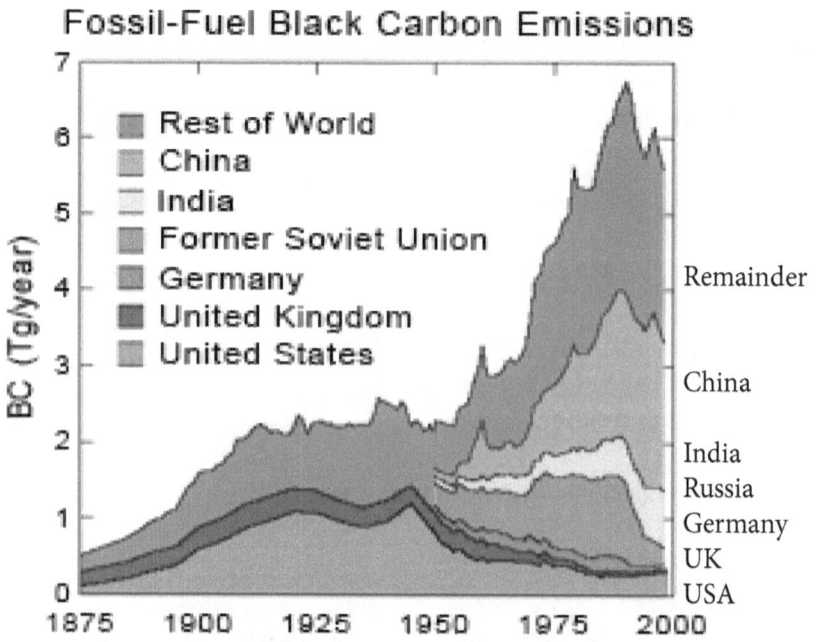

China now emits more mercury than the United States, India, and Europe combined[1]. China and India together account for 25-35% of global black carbon emissions[2] Black carbon emissions from China doubled from 2000 to 2006.[3]

The database below is from a compilation put together by the World Health Organization (WHO) in 2011, for all the cities with PM10 measurements since 2008. This denotes the Top 33 Cities with the Worst Air Quality in the World.

Data is annual average PM10 concentrations in micro-gm/m3.

Notice the cities in India and China present within this data.

There now exists real-time AQI (air quality index) readings in India and China. On the date I am writing, air quality in Beijing is denoted as "unhealthy" with regards to particulate matter/soot emissions whereas the worst city in the United States is "moderate".

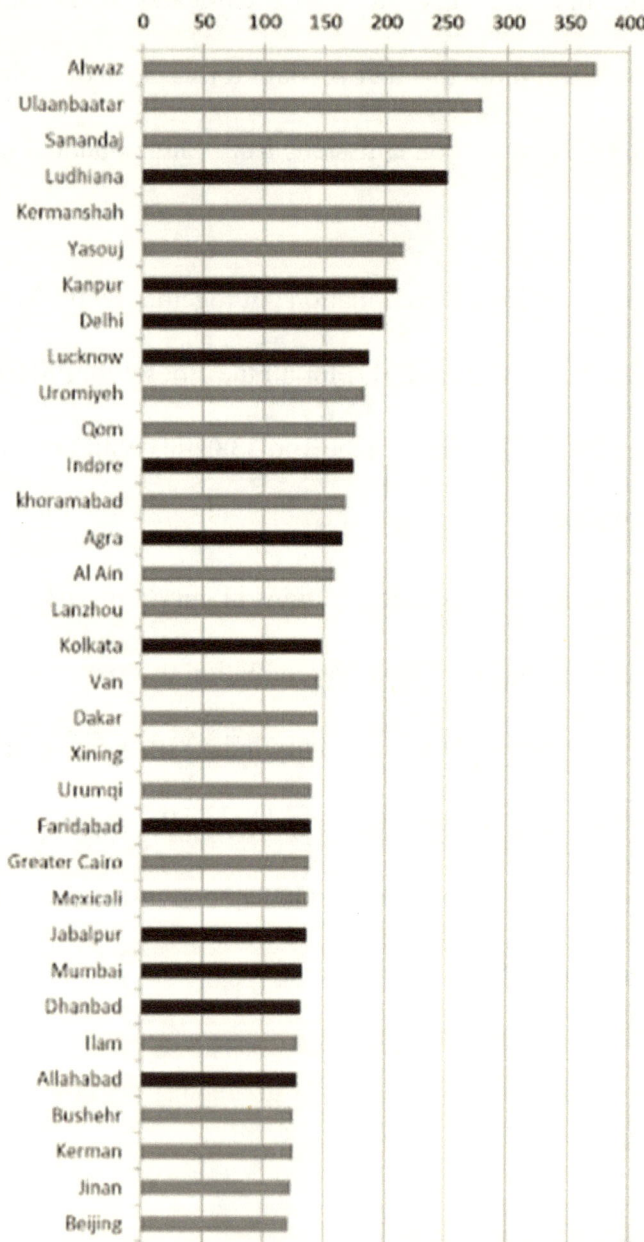

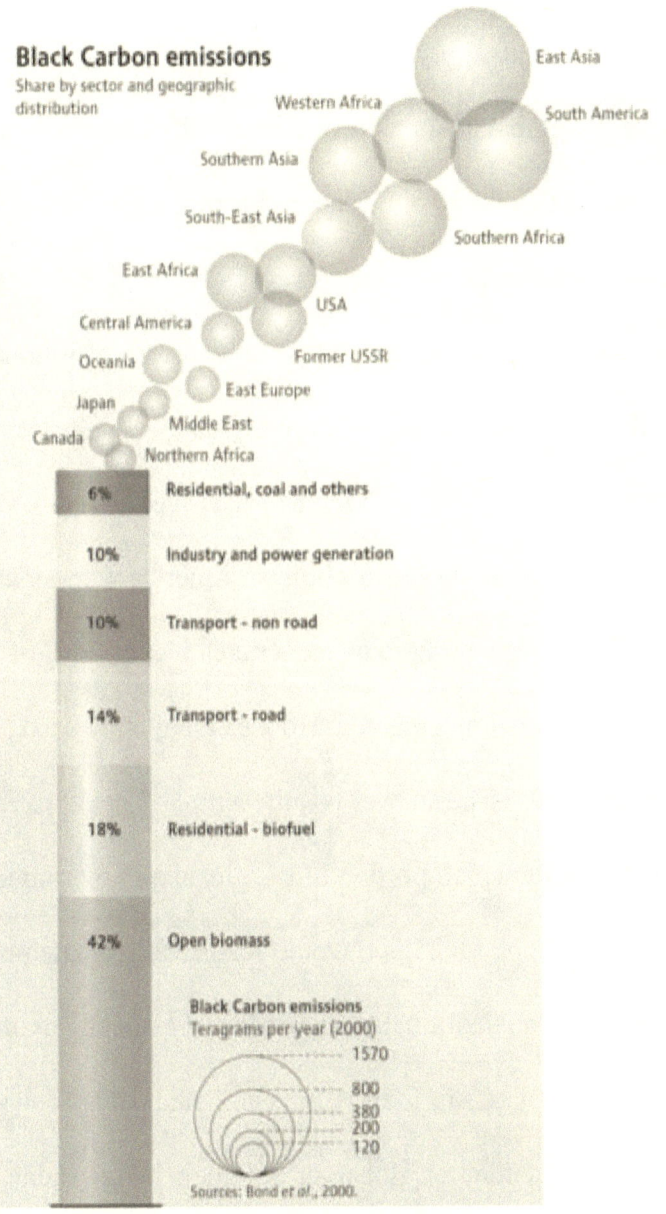

Black Carbon emissions

Share by sector and geographic distribution

East Asia

Western Africa

South America

Southern Asia

Southern Africa

South-East Asia

East Africa

USA

Central America

Oceania

Former USSR

Japan

East Europe

Canada

Middle East

Northern Africa

6%	Residential, coal and others
10%	Industry and power generation
10%	Transport - non road
14%	Transport - road
18%	Residential - biofuel
42%	Open biomass

Black Carbon emissions
Teragrams per year (2000)

1570
800
380
200
120

Sources: Bond et al., 2000.

www.skepticalscience.com

Are we crippling our economy in America by self-sacrifice, while other countries and nations continue to create pollution at exponentially greater levels? Have we forgotten to apply common sense to our decision making? Would it not serve our global health care and air quality better to implement standards in all nations to adhere to the same standards of America? Is it truly logical that we can accept 2 ppm (parts per million) of PCB's in fish that is sold for consumption, while we want to restrict soot emissions to .25 ppb (parts per BILLION)? By the way, a campfire emits a higher level of soot emissions than .25 ppb – just for reference. The supremely ironic realization of implementing higher restrictions in America with regard to soot emissions, is that we are going to create a much higher level of global air pollution if this is implemented. How can that be you ask, if we are lowering our emissions? The answer is quite simple. The air over America represents a rather small portion of the global air environment. While reducing from .75 ppb to .25 ppb would realistically create no recognizable benefit to global air quality, increasing the already exorbitant-ly high levels of soot emissions in India, China and other Asian countries creates a much higher potential for global air pollution. While India, China and other countries will continue to pollute the air at soot levels in excess of 3 ppb, these levels will grow even more if manufacturing pulls out of America to escape our stricter standards. Greater quantities of coal would be exported to China for example, if the demand to burn coal in America is eliminated or substantially reduced. These quantities will be burned in factories that continue to emit soot at the higher levels. Therefore, globally our air quality will suffer at the same time our economy in the U.S. suffers. It would be akin to eliminating automobiles in our country, returning to horse and buggy – to lower emissions in America. While the reduction in emissions might be recognized, so would the departure of business, manufacturing, transportation and economic development. Business cannot lose focus of the primary goal by focusing on a secondary or tertiary goal.

Consider the minimum wage discussion and pending legislation. There is an effort to increase minimum wage in our country. In 1971, minimum wage was $2.65/hr and in 1989, minimum wage was $3.35. What strikes me as odd during this 21-year span of only a $.70/hr increase – is that during the next 20 years – minimum wage was increased $3.90/hr! From different surveys, the percentage of employees earning minimum wage is 4-5%! Considering the majority of wage earners at the minimum wage level are either entry-level employees or non-skilled, perhaps it is fair that minimum wage be fixed at a much lower level. Does a high school student at his first job honestly deserve $7.25/hr – much less the $9+/ hour that is being considered? It seems rather ludicrous to raise minimum wage to create a positive effect for 4-5% of the workforce – while thereby negatively affecting 100% of the American workforce! To decrease the discretionary spending of all citizens trying to appease a small percentage of employees that perhaps are lesser paid, is this truly logical and the best solution? It would appear that increasing minimum wage will result in smaller businesses having to layoff workers, slowing our economic growth, raising high school drop-out rate, creating more competition for fewer jobs and of course reducing discretionary spending for EVERY consumer!

Is disparity of income a bad thing? Labor costs have significant implications toward a business' sustainability and profitability. Many businesses maintain a strict percentage of labor cost for their operation. Why should those citizens that fail to work hard, educate themselves, learn valuable skills – be rewarded by increased wages? The greater travesty is that employers having to pay higher wages for their least skilled employees, will no longer be able to pay their more valuable and skilled employees a higher wage that they legitimately deserve! After all, businesses must be profitable and can't be faulted for managing their expenses to not only survive, but also grow.

Those citizens that have worked hard, excelled in the workplace, have obtained skills and education to meet their job requirements and succeed – need to realize that increases in minimum wage will only serve as lack of pay increases for themselves.

In some cases, government can assist our nation in developing business and industry. Unfortunately, government can also destroy business and industry - many times before it can be established. The dreams of Henry Ford almost never came to fruition, because of government and legal implications. A few votes could have stopped the automotive boom, before it began. However, the primary concern at the time was the trial of Standard Oil and J.D. Rockefeller - and the government's efforts to squash the monopoly of the oil & gas industry. It was deemed that Rockefeller had cornered the market for oil & gas, along with becoming too powerful and wealthy for others to compete. The government did rule that Standard Oil would be divided, eliminating this monopoly and reducing the power and wealth for Rockefeller. In the end, Rockefeller retained approximately a 25% share in all of the subsidiaries and subsequently attained even greater wealth, to the point of being the wealthiest man in America. It also resulted in increased costs for American citizens, similar to the efforts of breaking up the telephone industry and Ma Bell.

In the end, consumers paid increased rates for phone service. Are these government decisions truly in the best interest of America? How can increased pricing be a good thing for Americans? Possibly the transition to wireless communication and "the cloud" would have occurred more rapidly, had this "monopoly" not been legislated to divide.

While my goal here is not to run for President or any political office, my advice is that businesses and industries not only need to educate themselves to legislation that negatively and positively affects their business, but also become an active role with their legislators in voicing their concerns and support. Remember what Pericles said…

Creativity and Innovation

I will step off my soap box for now, as I tend to become passionate when discussing areas of improvement for economic growth. I remain optimistic and encouraged at the results I have seen recently of new manufacturing and the return of existing manufacturers to America. One of my self-imposed goals is to recruit an OEM automotive manufacturer to our local community. With manufacturers in our area already capable of producing automotive subframes, wiring harnesses, steering wheels, airbags, cables, automotive panels and trim, tires, etc… it seems a logical fit for our community to attract such a manufacturer. Upon reflection, perhaps there is an option to create our own automotive plant. While entertaining the notion might seem ludicrous, I have witnessed much more amazing accomplishments in the recent months. My manufacturing career has primarily been automotive related, which stimulates all these "ideas" in my mind related to automobiles. I think of an advance warning system for emergency vehicles which would override your stereo system, providing an audible alert before an emergency vehicle is upon you. I wonder if it would be possible to implement electromagnetic brakes on automobiles, eliminating the need to replace brakes constructed of friction material (and hoses, cylinders, fluid, etc..). I wonder why with a substantial portion of the costs of automobiles lying within the amortization of tooling used in the manufacture of steel frame components, castings, etc… why don't the drive train and frame remain the same for 10-15 years with only interchangeable bodies to attach to the frame. This would also serve to reduce repair costs and insurance costs theoretically as well. With regard to reducing insurance costs, why aren't the front and rear subframes of automotive vehicles collapsible into the main seating compartment frame of the vehicle? It could allow for either pneumatic, hydraulic or even spring-loaded cylinders to allow for compression of the front and rear subframe into the middle frame. It would seem that crashes 15 mph and less might sustain very limited or no damage. Sure, there would have to be allowances for cables, columns, braces, hoses and tubing to accept this compression scenario as well – but I would suspect that wouldn't be much of a challenge for an engineer. Possibly the best idea is to design some prototypes and print on a 3D printer.

It boggles the mind to consider what changes will be evident in just the next decade. 3D printers and "show and tell" robots are just the beginning. I picture "employee-less" grocery stores in the future. Deliveries made to these grocery warehouse by suppliers, with suppliers offloading their deliveries onto conveyors that transport the items to specific refrigerated or dry storage areas of the warehouse. With the advent of robotics and   automated picking machines, do we not think it is possible to place an order via our pad or smartphone to pick items we want and have them waiting when we arrive? Upon the scanning of our debit/ credit card – the order would be released from its appropriate refrigerated and dry storage locations and conveyed to our pick-up point.

However, creativity and innovation don't always imply "new" processes, machinery, equipment or inventions. Creativity and innovation can simply be applying existing technology, equipment or processes to new applications. A company was experiencing bottlenecks at substations within their plant. Production runs were segregated into batch runs of anywhere from 200-500 pcs. Each work station required deliveries of product and subsequent component parts to produce a final product. The bottleneck was created due to a lack of material handlers to constantly setup these work stations with product and supplies. With such small batch quantities and a limited number of forklift drivers, there was consistent waiting at work stations for the next setup of materials. While supervisors and managers were considering the costs of additional forklifts, forklift driver certification, additional forklift drivers, etc..., one of the operators suggested a very simple solution. A local grocery store had closed down and their shopping carts were for sale - CHEAP! By utilizing shopping carts, each operator could retrieve their own parts, additional component parts and deliver to their workstations. Subsequently they could move this finished product via the shopping carts to the next work station or packaging/shipping. The storage of these empty carts, as we all know, is a breeze - with carts collapsible and stackable within one row. How simple but yet how brilliant? This creative, innovative solution eliminated potential forklift safety concerns, additional forklift drivers & certifications and delays in changeovers. The ability to recognize that existing technology could be utilized in a different environment resulted in cost savings and safety improvements.

 If Chris Anderson is correct and our country is truly on the brink of a new industrial revolution, just imagine how incredible our future will be with our young people implementing sound business principles, learning technical skills, reaching out globally to educate themselves and having faith in their ideas. Don't be afraid to use your own judgment, don't get distracted by issues that take you "off task" and most importantly – don't be afraid to ACT even if it fails. It has been said that we will never know the inventions and miracles that failed to be realized, because someone gave up the brief moment before success.

Consider the discoveries of Thomas Edison, Alexander Graham Bell, Benjamin Franklin, Christopher Columbus, Eli Whitney and others. Would these have ever been recognized if these people had given up? Many inventions and discoveries are the result of an individual's critical thinking skills and intuitive nature. We have faced a rather difficult economic climate during the past 8-10 years. However, I truly believe we are ONE invention away from economic growth. In the same way that railroad, oil & gas, steel, electricity and automobiles made America the global economic superpower during their time, the next great invention in America can have the same effect. All it takes is one invention that has a global impact, along with an effective business leader to promote it. We are waiting on our next Vanderbilt, Rockefeller, Carnegie, Edison, Tesla, Westinghouse, Ford, J.P. Morgan: the question is "who will emerge as the next leader to kick-start our economy?"

I am aware that many businesses and industries widely promote the "team approach". For many businesses and industries, this approach is successful and desirable. However, don't forget that individual accomplishments often times result in the best ideas and solutions. It would be foolish if we only considered the results of a majority consensus or team-approach to all problem resolution. The patent process itself conflicts with the belief that all new concepts and discoveries should be based upon a consensus or team approach. Teams work effectively for some things, individual efforts work effectively for others. Simply don't allow your perception of one method to be more valuable than the other.

Is the "team" approach always the best way? I was serving in a management position in an automotive related manufacturing facility, when an initiative swept industry to create a "team" approach to business. In retrospect, those having the most difficulty in adjusting to this team approach were supervisors and managers who had previously not relinquished authority and power to subordinates. The "team" approach had positive merits. It allowed for workers to be more involved in decision-making, giving them a vested interest in the company and results obtained. The new approach typically improved employee morale as teams were allowed to hire and fire within their group, to be responsible for disciplinary actions and to set goals and objectives for the group. In aggregate, the team approach made a lot of sense. Just as the most accomplished sports teams are not successful without stellar efforts from the entire team, the concept of successful business relied on this same premise. In football, there is no one expert that is proficient in running, passing, kicking, punting, tackling, blocking, etc.... Neither in business is there one expert proficient in sales, engineering, accounting, supervising, maintenance, etc.... Both sports and business require that a successful team be formed to include specific individuals proficient in a specific area, but working together effectively as a "team" for a common goal.

However, just as many concepts and ideas – the reality of implementation was flawed and failed to create positive results in all cases. Teams were now handling hiring, firing, disciplinary action – however team members were not trained nor educated to the skills required to enact these directives. Of particular concern was the legal ramifications of incorrectly interviewing, disciplining and firing individuals. Teams would make spending decisions in relation to new processes, new equipment or machinery, new methods of tracking production and quality, etc.... Once again, these teams however could not accurately calculate a return on investment, amortization of equipment and tooling, recognize effects to costs and efficiencies. For these reasons, many businesses and industries quickly abandoned the team approach. It is absolutely true that "teams" should not be allowed to lead all projects or even have input into every decision. The majority will NOT always make the correct decision. If everything relied on a majority approval or a team to make a decision, think of all the things that would NOT have happened in this world.

Perception is NOT reality

In mentioning the word perception, whoever coined the phrase "perception is reality"is clearly misled. Perception is often times not even closely related to reality. Think of recent worldwide events. It was assumed or perceived that Saddam Hussein would be protected by his many guards, possibly locked in one of the reinforced lower basements within one of the complexes he frequented. Reality however, was the Hussein was found in rural farmland in a hole simply covered by a sheet metal covering – no guards, no alarm systems, no reinforced walls, etc… Ironically, it was equally assumed that Bin Laden would be found hiding out in a cave in the mountainous regions of Afghanistan or Pakistan – hiding in seclusion. However, Bin Laden was in a populated town region in a multi-story complex living with wives, kids, guards, etc…. From years ago when perception was that the world was flat and subsequently proved round by Christopher Columbus, one thing has remained certain – perception is NOT reality! Therefore your perceptions of what might be successful in business and industry could quite honestly be totally opposite to ideas and changes that prove to be positive. For any familiar with the "Letters to the Editor" section in newspapers or any site that allows for blogging, I'm sure you are equally amazed at how far from reality people's perceptions lie. In my community, and probably in yours too, people will write or post comments such as "our community has higher taxes than any community" or " industry gets all the tax breaks and they don't pay their fair share" or "we waste money on potential manufacturing sites, when we need to spend money on our current financial requirements" or "our state has the highest poverty rate of any state". What citizens fail to realize is that by posting negative comments in newspapers and blogging on websites, it creates the self-fulfilling prophecy that their community is failing. What business wants to relocate to an area that has all these problems? Businesses and industries are hesitant to move to a community where it is perceived they would encounter all these problems. Our community has not been immune to such negative propaganda either. Never mind that we are taxed less than many states and the majority of counties within our state. Never mind that one industry in our community pays in property taxes an equal amount as 350 average homes in our community. Never mind that we "wasted" SPLOST (special purpose local option sales tax) money on industrial property, but within a few years recruited a 1.5 million square ft facility that employs over 700 citizens within our region. Never mind that our poverty rate is not the lowest. Ironically, the state to which a recent politician compared us, stating we should follow their lead – has a poverty rate far in excess of our state's. Why then do people not recognize that statements and opinions should be backed by facts, figures and data? These same people that claim industry should pay more taxes, fail to realize their efforts will repel prospective industries. The net effect of this will be that residential and small business WILL have to pay more in taxes, due to the lack of tax revenue from these manufacturers. Keep in mind these large industries pay an exponentially larger portion of school taxes as well. In the end, negative comments that are successful in repelling industries, will only serve to raise the taxes for the community and/or lower the revenue for education and governmental services. For those of you that truly dislike your community, do the community a favor and simply leave. Your efforts to complain in the interest of bettering the community only serve to sabotage your community. The same holds true for business. If employees complain publicly about the company being such a terrible place to work, their perceived poor treatment of employees, suppliers or customers – these complaints only serve to damage the employer.

This same discussion could have been presented in the "ethics of business" chapter! Without suppliers and customers, the business fails and the employee loses employment. An employee's perception of their employer is many times no more accurate than a citizens perception of their community.

While this applies more your company as a whole and your community, how can misperception affect your business internally? All of us have experienced the worker deemed as unambitious or lazy. How is this dealt with in companies? In some cases, the difficult tasks and/or important tasks are not assigned to these workers. The reason being these employees can't or won't contribute as much as your more energetic employees. However, is this reality? I have witnessed the following: **give your most difficult job to your laziest person and they will find the easiest way to do the job!** Could it be that laziness is a positive attribute? Why do we have power tools rather than manual? Why do we prefer to drive or fly instead of walk? Why do we want to access everything on smartphones and tablets? Could it be that laziness is an equal driver to innovation as cost? Our society is driven as much by convenience as cost. We sometimes to prefer to classify this as comfort rather than laziness. Is that because the word laziness simply has a negative perception?

Be open to new ideas

There are certain basic premises that determine the success and growth of business and industry. Expenses cannot exceed sales. Defective and discrepant product can destroy a business. Business must be providing a product that is in demand. Ethics must be adhered to when running any business, as legal issues can quickly put one out of business. Once again, just because something is legal doesn't mean it is ethical. Don't lose focus of these basic needs for business sustainment and growth, while exploring new technology, software changes, MRP/ERP systems, different methods of running your business (LEAN, Six Sigma, Team-based environment, etc…). Not every method nor idea applies to every business. It is important to choose the methods that specifically apply to your business environment, don't try to "fit" new concepts into your business simply because it has worked for others (reference KANBAN's don't work for all inventory management situation).

I believe most people understand today that the Japanese concepts that led to the industrial revolution in Japan were in reality, introduced by an American. As a previous manager for three (3) Japanese manufacturers, I was constantly exposed to the ideas of "plan,do,check,act", designing quality into the process, applying statistic process control, implementing technology and determining root causes of problems. These concepts were introduced to the Japanese by W. Edwards Deming. Deming is credited for the launch of the Total Quality Management philosophy, although not specifically denoted as TQM in his teaching or books. Japan was receptive to the ideas of this American during a time when America was not equally as receptive. Recognizing that we are not a global economy, we need to learn from this experience and be receptive into philosophies and ideas from all over the world. It is a shame I had to learn from the American W. Edwards Deming during visits to Japan.

I have traveled to Japan on multiple occasions, training with two separate large Japanese manufacturers. In addition to becoming a rock star in karaoke bars and losing weight during the trips, I accomplished a few intended goals as well. The primary purpose of the visits were that each company was to train me in their operations, their management style, their supply chain management, product awareness and to create networks for support – I found myself learning an equal amount of knowledge from observations made at facilities in Japan. These unintended benefits of the trips proved to stir ideas and process to implement, that would create benefit for our business in America. Many of the best ideas proved to be extremely simplistic and basic in nature. "red card/green card example vs our computer notification method of tracking receipts and shipments".

Similar to this very basic and non-technical method of monitoring

receipts and shipments, certain operations were very manual. At the time

we were implementing robots for welding at our North American facility,

there was no effort in certain areas to implement robots in the Japanese

facilities. While we were attempting to achieve "paperless" status in our

North American facility, the Japanese relied heavily on spreadsheets and

documents that consumed enormous quantities of paper. I had incorrectly

"assumed" that the Japanese were dependent upon technology in many

more aspects of their business than America. What did I say earlier about

perception NOT being reality?

Japanese are known to be very respectful, hard-working and dedicated to

their cause. Ironically after being so receptive to American thinking during

the period of reconstruction in Japan, I noticed that there appeared to be an

attitude of dismissal upon hearing of new ideas at the American facilities.

To relate this resistance to better ideas and to also emphasize the reliance

on "paper" rather than technology, let me provide a brief example.

Within the American facilities of these Japanese-owned companies, there

is typically a Japanese manager ranked slightly above the American man-

ager. In the need for resolution, the Japanese manager would have the right to final decision. For those American managers that had never relinquished their rights to decision-making, this became a difficult transition into the Japanese manufacturing culture. Admittedly, many Japanese felt a difficult transition having to explain themselves to an American manager. After all, it was a Japanese company and the Japanese were providing us (Americans) jobs. I was EXTREMELY fortunate to have an excellent working relationship with my Japanese manager. Jun was not only extremely knowledgeable and dedicated to the company, but more importantly was refreshingly open-minded to listen to suggestions and ideas from me – his American counterpart/subordinate. Jun would arrive early each morning, revisit detailed plans each day for goals, issues and results. However I noticed Jun would stay at work until 9-10 p.m. every night. I just wasn't certain of the purpose for these late hours. As Jun and I began to become more acquainted, we discussed activities outside of work (softball, golf, movies, shopping, tourist attractions, etc…). While Jun eluded to a strong desire to involve he and his wife in the community and extracurricular activities, his work schedule did not allow for this. I simply asked Jun, "why do you have to work so late every night?" I still remember my shock as Jun described for me his efforts each night to resolve daily production, schedule changes, purchasing adjustments, etc…. While we utilized an MRP system to record production, generate a production

schedule, generate purchase orders/releases, track inventory – I found

that Jun's process for calculating future needs and adjustments relied on

the printing of reports from the system, then manually matching data

between numerous reports to determine future requirements. So I asked

Jun, "Why don't you simply run these as queries and use Excel or Ac-

cess to calculate the desired results?"" No, No, No, that is

unacceptable. We don't trust calculations in software outside of our

system" was his response. I protested to no avail that the data was

pulled directly from the system, so the results could be trusted as

determined by whichever outside software he chose to use (i.e. Excel,

Access). While normally receptive to other ideas, Jun was adamant

that this was not an option and could not even be considered – since

this was not a method approved by the company. I was dumbfounded

that this extremely intelligent man felt that scrolling visually through

three (3) separate spreadsheets and reports, comparing results from

each, manually calculating differences and manually writing down

these new requirements – could possibly be more accurate than allow-

ing the computer to perform this work?! I asked Jun to allow me to

run a trial with him for the week. He could use his manual method to track changes, new requirements, record data while I used my method for determining the same information. If I could prove to him that my results were 100% accurate, would he be willing to consider my method? This is exactly what we did. The first night Jun ran his reports, printed and began sifting through the information to calculate and determine changes and requirements for the next day's/week's production. I downloaded the same reports to a text file, pulled up in Microsoft Excel and generated links to a new Microsoft Access database I created to use for the project. I then created my formulas in the Access database to automatically calculate results and filter out the results I needed to review (anything negative – with regard to sales filled, finished goods inventory/raw materials/com-ponents/packaging). Please keep in mind that the first night I had to create the download links, create the new spreadsheets and create the new database along with these formulas. After the first night, I simply had to run these links and the database that I created. Even with considerably more time than subsequent nights, I finished running my information THREE (3) HOURS prior to Jun finishing! In the end, we began to compare information to confirm the results were the same. This took a considerable amount of time as Jun's information was random, not sorted by part number nor value nor description. My information obviously could be sorted by any column value or row. We found two (2) discrepancies

during the next couple of hours of checking results – an omission by Jun

or a miscalculation. While I could tell that Jun was obviously impressed,

he still informed me that without equally impressive results for the entire

week – he would not consider using my method. During the next four

days, we ran through the scenario every evening. Jun would take any-

where from 2-3 hours to perform these same tasks he had been performing

for the past 5 years, while I honestly completed my portion in less than

15 minutes from start to finish. I have to admit I honestly acted like I was

still working on the data for an additional 30 minutes or so, just to avoid

embarrassment for Jun. By the end of the week, I had a new best friend!

Not only was Jun able to leave work within an hour after the end of pro-

duction, but he was able to begin playing softball on the company softball

team and he also began playing golf in the evenings! I have failed to see a

happier Japanese man than one who is allowed to play golf multiple times

in a week! Keep in mind, in Japan they sometimes have to make "tee

times" for driving ranges. The cost of playing golf in Japan is so

prohibitive that many Japanese are able to fly to Hawaii and play golf,

cheaper than playing in their homeland. Not only did this man reduce

his working hours, but subsequently became more accurate in his work, while at the same time improving his quality of life! Why did this happen? Because an individual was open-minded to change, didn't resist change and was accepting of a subordinate – albeit a foreigner. I readily admit that many Americans are equally as proud in the American way being the best way or the only way. Many hesitate to accept foreign ideas and foreign cultures. If we are truly to thrive in a global economy, we must be open-minded to global concepts and ideas.

I have to admit I did not welcome all Japanese concepts. I like my fish cooked, I don't want to eat horse, and raw eggs for breakfast are not my personal favorite. When I want to eat pizza, I want it to be pizza with dough, marinara, cheese and possibly some "cooked" meat and/or vegetables. For those of you confused by this statement, pizza in Japan means a bowl of seafood, egg, seaweed, etc…which you mix together and cook on a grill (kind of like a seaweed/seafood omelet). In all honesty, I should probably be more receptive to their cuisine as well. The Japanese life expectancy exceeds that of Americans. While it is not required to accept the cuisine of foreign countries, we only harm ourselves if we are not accepting of foreign countries and their contributions to America. Gone are the days that "Buying American" means only buying Ford, GM or Chrysler vehicles. Ford, GM and Chrysler produce vehicles and components globally as do Toyota, Honda, Hyundai, Kia, Mercedes, BMW, Volvo and Nissan. The latter companies -Toyota, Honda, Hyundai, Kia, Mercedes, BMW, Volvo and Nissan have a huge presence of manufacturing in America. This same comparison can be made to the Tier I, Tier II and Tier III suppliers for these companies. These suppliers have also located facilities globally to support the OEM's. If the desire is truly to experience economic growth, reduce unemployment and improve our quality of life in America – it is incumbent upon us to support those companies that have chosen to locate in America, employing its citizens.

Seek creativity and skills at an early age

What created this desire in my mind to learn how things operated? Why was I a "geek" in my younger years, that wanted to figure out how everything operates? I realize that some kids were playing with G.I. Joes during the time I was building radios, transmitters, photo sensor lights with my Radio Shack 100 projects in 1 kit. Even with basic toys such as Lego's, I was never satisfied until I created something abnormal from the typical creations. Possibly my Dad stimulated this interest in me. After all, I'm sure it was not my mother's idea to buy me a Radio Shack 100 projects in one kit. My Dad himself had built a large stereo from a Heathkit, that included a reel-to-reel player, tuner, turntable all wrapped in large wooden cases with separate "large" speaker enclosures. My Dad always seem to be interested in the latest technology, whether the first VCR ($800) of any of my friends or "surround sound" before it was commonly sold to the American consumer. My Dad built "surround sound" into our living room by cutting holes in the ceiling to install custom-built speakers, built a sub-woofer and connected all of this through our TV via a stereo tuner and cables running through walls and the attic. While I personally loved it, apparently my mother wasn't so excited about this project. This was not, however, the project my mother despised

the most. Referencing back to the creative side of my Dad and I, I would

be remiss if I didn't reference the Pontiac truck that I drove during high

school. I know what you are thinking, Pontiac didn't build a truck. You

would be correct, Pontiac didn't build a truck but my father and I did!

Honestly my mother was justified in her hatred for this project. Basically

my mother and father picked out my first vehicle to drive. Granted, I was

going to have to share it with my mother which explains why I was not

involved in selecting the vehicle. Trust me, a 16 yr old boy does NOT

select a Pontiac Catalina for his first vehicle. It is not exactly a "babe

magnet" nor is it cheap on gas. None of that was a consideration of my

mother, who was really pleased to "give" me this 4 door, gas guzzler (400

cu in engine) with white vinyl seats. My mother did take special pride in

her new car and to be honest, I was honestly very appreciative just to

have a vehicle to drive. That special sense of pride in the car changed for

my mother early one Saturday morning. I was picking up some friends

of mine to go play in a charity volleyball tournament. During this time in

my life, I worked very late at a local restaurant to earn extra money. Okay,

actually it was to earn enough money just to fill up the tank of the

Pontiac. Nonetheless, on this fateful Saturday morning I was very sleepy and apparently fell asleep driving to one of my friend's house. I woke up as the first mailbox hit the windshield as I was riding through a ditch. While falling asleep, apparently I pressed down the gas pedal and accelerated. I overcompensated trying to bring the vehicle back onto the road, clearing the road on the other side. Two more mailboxes, one ditch and a power pole later I came to rest with the vehicle on the side in a ditch. I could hear screams, but luckily it was not somebody that I had injured. It was however, a nice lady who had decided to sit on her front porch and read the morning paper. Crawling out of the vehicle, I noticed the damage on the vehicle as I had attempted to swerve to avoid striking the power pole head-on. I did manage to steer the front of the car clear, but the entire back half of my Mom's prized Pontiac was crushed beyond recognition. After the vehicle had been towed back to my house and lowered into the yard, I became aware that my parents were not investing in the purchase of another vehicle. I honestly couldn't blame them, as I had pretty much totaled this vehicle within a couple of months of driving it. However, if I was to continue driving, it became evident that the Pontiac would have to be resurrected from the dead. Therein became the concept of my father and I to build the Pontiac Cruck (car/truck). Yes my friends called it other names like the Pontiac Sandbox or the Pontiac Catbox (a derivative of the Catalina name). While not aesthetically appealing, our creation did satisfy the need of basic transportation. I never realized how complicated it was to cut a car in half, remove the back half and subsequently construct a truck body onto what was the rear of a beautiful car. It was also a unique concept to drive a vehicle that was ½ metal and ½ wood, granted not a great concept. For my participation, I was much more comfortable in wood-working skills than metal-working skills. My Dad was proficient with a cutting torch, welder and Bondo. I was more confident in cutting boards, driving nails and painting. The reward from this experience was not in the look of my new "exclusive" ride. I mention exclusive because my mother no longer wanted to share a vehicle with me. The reward from this experience was that I was able to work with my Dad almost every single evening and weekend. Looking back, I can only imagine how much my father did not feel like working on this vehicle! My Dad worked long hours and deserved time at home to rest. Instead, he would come home, change clothes and we would begin cutting, welding, wiring, etc…. to create something together. During this time I learned technical skills   related to design, electrical, hydraulic, metal-working, glass cutting (back window) and painting. Yes I learned many of these skills through mistakes and failures, requiring rework and repeating of operations. However, these mistakes served as an important learning experience related to quality control and efficiencies. To incur additional costs (on a limited budget) for materials and waste time for rework is a painful process for a 16 yr old. I suspect my manufacturing employers over the years are glad that I was exposed to these painful lessons before working for their applicable companies. My concern is these lessons aren't learned anymore by young people. This project was probably the worst project in my life, while also the best project of my life. I ran into numerous roadblocks, things didn't work, the project ran longer than I expected, the costs were more than budgeted, I had to learn new ways to achieve the goal, etc.....

(The Pontiac truck, what I "thought" was impressive at 16 yrs old)

It is seemingly similar to the way Steven Spielberg references the making of "Jaws"[6]. The mechanical shark broke every day, the project ran over the timeline by months and costs were far more than budgeted and he was at the risk of losing the movie and probably any future job in the movie business. It forced Spielberg and the writers to adapt to the situation and create the story without the shark appearing in most scenes. In the end, Jaws was the largest-grossing box office movie of its time and allowed Spielberg to basically direct any movie he wanted moving forward.

These similar struggles that I faced (on not such a grand scale) required that I "adapt" my project, implement cost-reduction ideas and develop new skills if I was ever going to drive again. Not only does it appear

that technical skills are not promoted as effectively with our youth,

but neither are the basic concepts of reducing waste and implementing

quality control checks. This basic understanding of technical skills can

be applied to multiple venues. Most are aware of 3D printers and the

implications of such technology. 3D printers utilize the same techni-

cal skills as other applications (i.e. – CNC programming, embroidery

digitizing, architectural design, laser cutting, etc…). The basic skill of

being able to understand and/or create designs which utilize x,y and z

coordinates, radii, circumference, lengths, angles, etc….. is vital to all

these computerized applications and more.

Network with businesses in your community

In my current position, I audit companies to ensure that waste is reduced, quality is enforced, process and technology advancements are pursued and an effective level of skilled workers are available in our industries. I have performed in excess of 75 audits during the past year in businesses and industries to assist in their efforts of sustaining growth and profitability. These audits are performed at new companies, Fortune 500 companies and smaller businesses that run the gamut of automotive, aeronautic, textile, food processing, packaging, distribution, machining, paper mills, ATV's, tires and agriculture. These audits combine efforts to identify needs for each applicable company whether related to logistics, supply chain, packaging needs, transportation needs, emissions, taxes, local and federal governmental regulations and workforce. In addition to these audits, industries are encouraged to participate in a industry con-sortium. The purpose of this consortium is to share ideas, voice common concerns and to present a unified voice for areas of similar support or opposition. Recently the governor in our state positively headed an effort to eliminate sales tax on energy used in manufacturing in our state. This obviously was received positively by manufacturing in the state, as we

were one of the few states that still enforced taxes on energy costs.

However, based upon the legislation that was passed – a local option was

available so that individual communities and municipalities (cities and

counties) could make the decision to implement an energy excise tax to

recoup the local portion of this sales tax. While the intent of this

legislation was to eliminate the competitive advantage neighboring states

held with regard to receiving expansions or recruiting new industry, now

this local option created a competitive advantage within cities and

counties within the state to retain companies, receive expansions for

existing industries and recruitment of new industry. I was tasked to act as

a liaison for both local government and industry to work together toward a

mutual decision toward whether to implement or exempt the local portion

of this energy sales tax. The consortium of manufacturers presented data,

facts and information related to the benefits of exempting the sales tax not

simply for the benefit of the company – but the effects these businesses

had on our communities with respect to the local small businesses they

supported, the number of local citizens they employed and of course the

local property taxes paid by these manufacturers. The cost savings

incurred by this energy sales tax exemption could be reinvested into the plants, thereby creating growth in some instances, ensuring that others sustain their business.

Manufacturers were intimately aware of the reduced tax revenue for our local governments and also well aware of the services and programs provided by local governments that supported their industries. Manufacturing was equally aware that reducing tax revenue could negatively affect some of these services and programs. Local government officials presented their information related to the decline in tax revenue, along with confirming the services and quality of life aspects that could be diminished if tax revenue was reduced. The respect for both sides was extremely impressive as considerations were given to solutions that would provide for an acceptable alternative for everyone concerned. I suspect resolution would not have occurred if all parties had not come to the table with respect and support for each side's agenda. Discussions were civil, pros and cons reviewed logically and methodically and in the end a decision was reached that both parties felt acceptable. While I mentioned previously that "team" decisions do no always yield the best decisions, this decision would not have been possible if members of both "teams" were involved. Choose the method of resolution and decision-making that is applicable to the situation!

Where did all the skilled workers go?

The most common concern expressed throughout manufacturing is the lack of available workforce! How can that be? After all, we read the media weekly stating high unemployment and that citizens can't find jobs. How is it possible with an increased level of unemployment that the primary concern for our industries is they can't find employees? The answer lies in the fact that these industries can't find qualified or experienced employees! From feedback I have received speaking at schools and colleges, most young people are either passion-driven, skills-driven or money-driven. For those passion-driven, these people feel a need to teach, heal or improve the lives of their fellow man through music and/or art. Skills-driven individuals have an existing skill in creating, building, designing, repairing or performing a task for which they have a natural or achieved ability to excel. Last are those that are money-driven, allowing a high potential income to drive their career choice. The ideal career is one you strongly desire, have the skills and knowledge to perform well and also pays well. Contrary to many people's perceptions, many technical jobs provide this career opportunity. The availability of technically skilled workers in our country is deficient. While 40-50% rates of retirement are fairly common place within the technically skilled jobs within the next 10 years, there appears to be a deficiency of filling the pipeline for these retiring employees with entry level employees skilled in the trades. Welders, pipefitters, electricians, maintenance technicians, PLC programmers, machinists, painters are skilled trades for which the lack of young people interested in pursuing these trades is creating a panic among manufacturing. What created this scenario? How can this be possible in a nation with over 8% unemployment, that employers can't find employees? As I considered the reasons for this deficiency in the skilled trades and asked for thoughts from hundreds of industries and educators, one of the answers is pretty simple – parents. Well now that I have offended engineers, I didn't want to leave out parents. Ironically during my conversations, I am the same parent as those that have failed to adequately educate our young people of the skilled jobs in demand. Granted if you are over 30, many of your parents worked in mills or in skilled trades. In earlier days these employees were not the high-wage earners, were not the highest educated and often were asked to perform dirty, nasty jobs. Remember I worked for manufacturing for over 20 years, so I have been covered head to toe in dirt and filth and earning a lower wage than some of the more professional career paths. While I don't recollect specifically steering my daughter away from the option of manufacturing, I also didn't direct her toward a path of manufacturing or a skilled trade. Possibly, that is why she obtained a degree in accounting. I remember my high school days and the students that chose the technical high school path. If I am being honest, many were considered lower aptitude with regard to their academic skills and once again the technical high school path led to lower paying jobs. I am concerned many other parents shared this same observation and failed to become educated to the advancements in these technical career paths. The tide has turned, job demand reversed and in many cases compensation scales have reversed with regard to technical vs traditional college paths. Now the CNC operator is earning more than the human resources administrator, the technician programming robots within the plant is earning more than the accountant in the office and tool and die repair technician is earning more than the safety coordinator for the facility. More importantly the demand for these skilled career paths is much greater than the traditional career paths. In our community, we have power plants, paper mills, 50+ yr old industries for which 40-50% of their employees will be retiring in the next 10 years! Electricians, welders, maintenance technicians, pipefitters, etc… are needed to replace these retiring employees – but there are not enough in the pipeline to fill the needs of our companies. In a recent speaking engagement at a local high school, one young man shared his story of obtaining his Bachelors degree in English, hoping to pursue a teaching career. His failure to find a teaching position led him to a 2 year technical certificate at the local technical college, which subsequently led to a well-paying position in the local electrical power utility company.

If expectations hold true and individuals are able to enter the manufacturing community at personal levels, to be effective not only will these people be responsible for the technical skills to create their business but also the ability to apply their ideas and creations into an effective business model. Consider an architect designing a skyscraper. Although educated and skilled in structural engineering, he would fail were it not for skilled builders that are competent and capable to bring the design to fruition. All planning and no follow-through creates zero results.

Not all advice is good advice

Not all advice is good advice! Some feel real estate investment is good, some advise to stay away from investing in real estate. During the past few years, many have declared bankruptcy based upon unwise real estate investments or poor financial decisions related to investment in real estate. I own rental property personally and have to admit that at times I have mixed feelings about the pros and cons of such an investment. I have suffered from property values falling during the past five (5) years as well, however it is like many investments – you have to remain for the long haul to recognize the benefits. For many, it has not been fiscally possible for them to retain their investments. I suspect in years to come, as these properties have been paid for, I will reap the benefits of this investment. Owning rental property has created ideas for inventions as well. Perhaps door locks for rental properties should be programmable by the landlords so that for the amount of rent paid, landlords can program accessibility to lock/unlock the doors to the premises. If a tenant can only pay ½ the months rent, the landlord simply programs in 15 days worth of access. It seems like a logical incentive for tenants to pay their rent, if they would truly be unable to access the premises. Yes I recognize the fact that there are legal implications that currently don't allow such an invention. Perhaps my next step is to address the legal issues.

Remember the statement, "perception is reality". While I don't consider this statement to be sound, I can think of many others. "You can't be their boss and their friend". "This stock is a great investment". Recently I was shocked at a technology and innovation seminar by a young entrepreneur. This young lady had developed a website to generate web traffic, for which businesses can subscribe to obtain feedback. While I commend this young lady for her technical skills in designing and creating the website and also commend her for supporting the U.S. economy with the creation of a business that will employee American citizens – I found myself shocked at some of her statements related to posting on the website. "Newspapers are outdated and on the way out" she declared. While I think it is important for news media to recognize the decline in population that reads printed newspapers, I could not totally disagree with this statement. But the statements to follow I found to be very concerning. "I base my decisions on what to purchase based upon comments I read in blogs". What? Seriously? I considered that comment for a moment, knowing full well I would almost NEVER base my decisions simply by reading the blogs of others. First, paid bloggers

submit postings on websites simply to promote their products and agenda.

The reference of a blogger to say that a car is "great" doesn't really per-

suade me to consider the purchase of a vehicle. This "great" vehicle could

get 10 mpg, have repetitive maintenance costs and incur high insurance

costs. I prefer to reference facts and data when considering the purchase

of an item. The speaker continued by stating "Don't worry about facts or

data when you post blogs on the site, the primary concern is just to start a

conversation"! WOW! It reminds me of the saying by Mark Twain

(substituting "blog" for newspaper):

"If you don't read blogs you are uninformed, if you do read blogs

you are misinformed"

Once again, I found this to be horrific advice to listeners in the audience.

Our country is struggling with false information, biased agendas,

apathy toward facts and figures when discussing legislation and ideas

along with the apparent lack of ethics and responsibility that should

accompany promoting your ideas and agenda to the public. While news

media spend an enormous amount of time validating sources, quotations,

facts, data and figures – this is the opposite of most persons posting blogs.

I do not think this speaker is evil or intentionally trying to mislead the public by such statements. I realize her agenda is to promote her website and to encourage participation, thereby generating a larger audience and thereby increased income. What I believe this speaker failed to realize is that she lacked the wisdom and knowledge to realize that her comments could create damage to our society and to our economy. While young, it appears she was highly unlikely to have experienced the negative repercussions of such comments. Just think of your typical postings on websites, noting the disparity of opinions and thoughts. If you've never read through comments about an article on "fracking", it presents a variety of strong opinions and advice towards the banning or growth of the fracking process. Not often are facts relayed in these postings, but I suppose blogs and posts do make for entertainment sometimes. But no more than I would base my decisions upon an animated entertaining movie, I would not base my decisions upon posted blogs. While there are those that exist that believe the priority is to start conversations, responsible parties believe in ensuring that facts and data support agendas, ideas and decisions.

Just as all advice is not good advice, similarly all business is not good business. As denoted by the title, there is an ever-present need to focus on the basic principles of business. The most basic of these principles requires that you take in more money than you spend. Eliyahu Goldratt increased awareness of "the goal" to making a profit[7], but sometimes it appears this concept is ignored by businesses and industries. Mr. Goldratt's book "The Goal" was the first common sense business book I read and was amazed at simple concepts that were ignored, primarily related to constraints and bottlenecks. At times it even appears the ultimate goal of making money is sometimes ignored. One of my previous employers accepted a new contract for supplying product to a new customer. Upon reviewing the pricing provided, it was apparent we were losing money on multiple part numbers. The method to the madness, as explained to me, was that we had to price these parts low because we would make up the difference by "volume" of the total list of part numbers quoted. While I understand this does happen from time to time, I expressed my concerns that this was not the best solution. My suggestion was that volumes be included in the contract to eliminate the opportunities for the customer to "cherry pick" the part numbers with low pricing, failing to purchase the part numbers for which we were profitable. This suggestion was ignored and I suspect you can guess the end result. As expected, we received substantial orders from the customer for numerous part numbers, all of which we produced at financial loss. How could a company be so blatantly blind to ignore the basic principle that income must exceed costs? Remember, there are just as many people inspired by ignorance as there are by brilliance! Many see the disastrous effects of a poor leader or poor process and create a plan or process to more effectively lead or produce. Many times the ideas inspired by ignorance actually serve to be more motivated than those inspired by brilliance! The need to create a better solution and avoid pain is a strong motivator – survival skills!

Exposure is knowledge

During my conversation with Chris Anderson, the subject arose of a trip that I took with my daughter during the week preceding and following her 16th birthday. We traveled to Europe for these weeks, visiting Italy, Austria, Hungary, Switzerland and France. I mentioned that the trip far exceeded expectations and that it stimulated my daughter's mind. However, I found myself struggling to explain to him the benefit of her visit to these countries and numerous cities. Sure, she became more interested in news stories, books and even movies that mentioned the cities and countries that she had visited. But was that truly the added benefit of our trip? I found myself realizing that simply by noticing beggars and poverty level citizens in some locations, ability to ride bullet trains, tours on natural gas-powered buses, seeing first-hand Versailles and learning the tragic history of its construction and effect on the nation of France, ability to view the vast array of artifacts and displays at the Louvre – riding subways in Paris, electric trolleys in Vienna, learning of the Austrian nuclear power plant that never opened,armed guards at certain borders and train stations, etc…, I realized that the biggest benefit of this trip was simply exposure. Exposure is both knowledge and power. Exposure allows for recognizing technology and being able to recognize applications for its use. Exposure is recognizing mistakes or failures that others have experienced, so that you don't follow the same paths. Exposure is increased awareness to poor government decisions. It allows for a proactive decision when you recognize trends that you suspect will turn out negatively, rather than waiting for the effects of poor policy. While my daughter may not fully recognize everything she experienced, she is a more knowledgeable and aware person simply because of exposure to different cultures and environments. She can form comparisons between her experiences in America versus what she has seen others experience in other countries. She can benchmark ideas and applications against those more successful ideas or advanced applications she has witnessed in other countries.

Exposure to your competition is equally as important to those that support your business. Recognize and respect your opposition! By no means does this insinuate that you should always agree with your opposition, but recognizing that your opposition can affect your business' success. It is important to understand your opposition. As the old saying goes "Keep your friends close and your enemies closer". Recognizing "frienemies" allows you to understand that working together creates a far more effective relationship than simply butting heads. The ability to compromise is not a symbol of weakness, but rather a symbol of strength. Anyone that has been married should be able to relate to this concept. This reminds me of Stephen Covey's – Focus on the issue, not the person[8]. Why do those people exist that exhibit personal anger when facing those with opposing opinions? Are we to believe that everybody that disagrees with our opinion is strictly disagreeing because of hatred for us? I am amazed at working relationships I have seen ruined because opposing opinions created such a conflict that the relationship was irrecoverable. Has not everyone of us reflected back to a past decision or action – and realized that we should have thought or performed in a better way? Why are we able to disagree with our own actions and thoughts, but yet are inflexible to disagree with others? In the same way we can benefit from opposing viewpoints, we can benefit from our competition. Is competition good or bad? The answer can be both. Healthy competition creates new ideas, new methods, new procedures, innovation, etc.... Unhealthy competition creates an environment where each party is simply focused on the competitive nature and winning against the competition, rather than focusing on their ultimate goal. We have all seen this as Democrats compete against Republicans for the simple purpose of appearing to be the winner over each other. The travesty is that while each party focuses on "winning" against the other party – our country suffers. An added challenge for legislators is the majority are prior lawyers - meaning they have been programmed to "WIN", rather than compromise. The same is true for departments competing against each other, managers competing against each other, union vs non-union labor, hourly vs salary. Many times the parties involved become so entrenched in their efforts to be better than their immediate competition, that they forget they should be recruiting their competition as allies to achieve both parties' common goals. Just as these separate parties create division in their respective organizations by losing sight of the common goals, efforts to understand each other and respect each other can lead to tremendous successes within their organizations.

Benchmarking

Regarding benchmarking, please ensure that you "benchmark" against those more advanced or successful than yourself. I realize most would view that as a foregone conclusion, but I have been amazed in my career at the efforts to benchmark against sister plants and other companies whose performance was actually inferior to our own! I have endured the "benchmarking' directives of inventory control at the previous company I referenced, for which we were confirmed to have the most accurate physical inventory in the history of the company for any plant location. Leading up to that, numerous discussions took place stating we need to benchmark and follow the procedures of the other facilities within our company. This directive to "benchmark" was led by an ineffective leader that showed no trust in his subordinates or confidence that his plant could possibly be the leader in this area of expertise. A different company also continually referenced "benchmarking" against a sister plant for the base of number of employees in a department, methods the sister plant used to order raw materials and components and the processes at the sister plant for filling customer demand via order completion. Once again, our management team endured these conversations of constant comparison to the other facility along with efforts to make us "conform" to the employment levels, ordering process and filling of customer orders. Thankfully the efforts of our managers prevailed. The end result is that we were able to manage departments with substantially less employees, achieved two (2) delivery awards from our customer (never achieved in the history of the plant) and eliminated shortages and expedite through our "created" system – while our sister plant continued to experience shortages and expedites utilizing the approved "system" at their plant. I am not a huge proponent of benchmarking. It just seems like you are attempting to "follow" rather than "lead". However, if you have difficulty in determining a best course of action and have humbled yourself to accept suggestions from others – make sure that you "benchmark" from leaders! Although I am personally hesitant to shamelessly copy even the leader, it makes absolutely no sense to copy those that are inferior.

Life isn't fair – sometimes the lucky win

Remember that life isn't fair. The smartest people aren't necessarily the highest paid (i.e. – the professional athlete reference), those deserving of respect don't necessarily receive it, the most talented persons don't necessarily secure careers in entertainment (reference any of the singing talent shows on TV), nor are the hardest workers rewarded for their efforts. Think of our tax system. Those that educate themselves, learn new and valuable skills, and work hard to achieve financial success – are penalized by taxation at a higher rate. Those individuals that make no effort to work hard, nor educate themselves nor learn skills are subsequently rewarded for their lack of effort – as taxed at a lower percentage. I still find it difficult to understand why it is not acceptable and fair to tax all working individuals at the exact same percentage. While I am definitely NOT a wealthy individual in this country, I find it extremely unfair that wealthy individuals are taxed at higher rates than those earning minimum wage. Which group is more likely to contribute to the sustainment and growth of our economy? Which is more likely to employ our nations citizens in their businesses? Is our goal to drive these type of individuals out of our country, so that other countries benefit from their knowledge, education, skills, work ethic and entrepreneurship? Wealthy citizens need to be treated with the same degree of fairness as poor citizens and taxed as an equal percentage of earnings. This would allow for those making more to pay more in taxes, but not at a higher rate than those earning minimum wage. Once again, life isn't fair. Perhaps one day logic will enter the picture and this unfair taxation will be reconciled. Can you achieve success purely by luck? Absolutely! There are those that win the Powerball, with jackpots into the millions of dollars. However, is it more likely to achieve wealth through education, working hard, wise investments OR waiting to win the lottery? I don't think many would be foolish enough to abandon logic and choose the lottery route. Reality dictates that many lottery winners are broke within a few years of winning these enormous jackpots. This confirms that those people that are not capable of managing finances and planning for their future, emphasizing that even the "lucky" need to be smart. I caught a world record fish when I was in high school. I was a novice at fishing. Honestly I walked across the road to a small private pond, simply for the purpose of practicing my casting technique. A friend was picking me up later to go fishing and I simply didn't want to be embarrassed by flaunting my "novice" skills at fishing. After a few casts from my Zebco 77, I felt a strong tug against my line and thought I had snagged some of the brush or weeds. No fish was jumping out of the water and there was just resistance as I continued to reel in my line. Then I saw the fish roll to the top of the water! Since I had caught very few fish in my life, I thought to myself "This is the largest fish I have ever caught". Granted, even at four (4) pounds this was the largest fish I had ever caught. I reeled in the fish, grabbed the bottom lip as I had seen on TV and walked the fish back home. The fish was still alive and I placed the fish in the bath tub to keep it alive. I wanted to show my friend when he came to pick me up, and a live fish would be much more believable than a dead fish I suspected. As my friend pulled into the driveway, I met him at his Jeep proudly stating I wanted to show him the fish I caught. He seemed rather uninterested but got out of his Jeep and walked with me into the house. When he saw the fish, he became VERY excited! He proclaimed "That is the biggest crappie I have ever seen in my life!". So there, I finally learned that the fish I caught was a crappie?! Even then, I didn't realize what that meant. However, through my friends encouragement I decided to find out if this was some sort of record. I had to weigh the fish on certified scales, measure the fish in numerous places and provide pictures, etc… related to the catch. Honestly however, I sent out the information feeling as though it was just a nice fish to catch. You can imagine how shocked to learn that articles of the catch appeared in sporting magazines, state and local newspapers and even catalogs for the lure used to catch the fish. Once again, it is NOT typical for somebody with no fishing skills and limited experience to catch a world record fish. The world record was issued for a 4 lb crappie for 10 lb line class and I believe still holds the record per the IGFA. Plain and simple, pure luck accounted for this success in my life. To catch a record fish with my fishing skills was about as likely as hitting a hole-in-one with my poor golf skills. However, that happened as well but that is a different story. I can tell you that my confidence in luck continuing to lead to success, was absolutely nil. I never expected to be a professional fisherman nor a professional golfer. I recognized that luck is unreliable and that to obtain a career, I needed to educate myself and learn skills that were in workforce demand.

This is the challenge for our young people today, identify the skills that are in workforce demand and learn them!

The art of dot-connecting

Although dot-connecting is not a skill typically listed on a resume, it is a skill that is an effective part of planning and managing business. To understand that involvement in your local technical college by assisting with input towards curriculum or even donating equipment/machinery can lead to training your future workforce, ensures filling the pipeline for the future. Recognizing that working with legislators to implement tax codes or exemptions beneficial to business, may serve to benefit your bottom-line at a time when you need it most. Becoming active in innovation and technology summits and/or communication may provide the application you need to become more competitive through lower labor costs, efficiency gains or improved quality. Participating in middle school and high school programs by supporting education lends itself to these students remembering your business in a positive way, which could lend to future employment for this young person or perhaps even a future customer for your business. Recently our community, like many, has faced a reduction in workforce of teachers. These cutbacks that affected teaching positions were created by reduced funding from the state level – applicable to education. While 46% of the state's budget is appropriated to education, tax revenue has declined. However, it has not simply been the recession that led to a decline in sales tax revenue. Internet sales have quadrupled during the past 5 years. These businesses didn't collect sales tax and therefore negatively affect the tax revenue for the state and local communities within our state. During 2012 alone, it is estimated that our state lost in excess of $832 MILLION in tax revenue. Repeating that 46% of the state budget is appropriated to education, this loss of tax revenue has had a devastating effect on education within the state. Granted, if citizens were aware that purchasing items via the internet could lead to a loss of teachers and an increase in the risk of lowering their child's education, I suspect that might change consumers minds about internet purchases. Once again, that requires connecting the dots. Luckily legislation at the state level was passed to require internet businesses to collect sales tax and return this tax to the state and local communities from which these purchases were generated. I am aware of an effort to pass this same   legislation at the federal level. The ability to connect the dots preemptively can avoid negative repercussions of business decisions as well. Businesses need employees with this skill.

No such thing as common sense

**"What fits your busy schedule better, exercising
one hour a day or being dead 24 hours a day?"**

I have resolved that there is no such thing as common sense. I mentioned

that I own rental property. I have been called to repair heating/air units

and found that the switch was simply turned to "off". I have been called

because the water would not shut off in the kitchen sink. When I arrived,

not only was the water still running full force (and of course I pay the

water bill), but the tenant had not considered simply reaching under the

sink to shut off the water cut-off valve. I'm sure you we can all reference

experiences where we find unbelievable reactions to simple problems.

Why does this reference to "common sense" deserve mentioning in a

book about basic business decision-making? The answer is because it is imperative to never assume individuals will follow the correct path. While this can create the negative results of "micro-managing" individuals, it more relates to communicating than managing. For business projects, focused tasks, customer requirements, employee implications – it is imperative that everybody is on the same page with the same goals with the same awareness. Effective communication is a critical tool for ensuring consistency within the group. However, this communication does NOT have to be verbal communication. Actually non-verbal communication is sometimes more reliable and accurate in business. Sometimes the best communication is NO communication! Yes I realize that many books have been written and sold, seminars taught and studies performed emphasizing the need to communicate EVERYTHING! So let me emphasize the importance of NOT communicating! Perhaps the basic lesson learned is to choose your battles. If your input will not change a decision of superiors and you know it, why risk your respect and possibly your job to make an argument that makes no difference? In addition, if someone that makes no decisions in the operation of your business but does however purchase goods or services from your business states something for which you totally disagree – is it really worth affecting your relationship with a customer to prove their position is wrong? Even in more subtle areas where employees feelings and security are at risk, what point is there in humiliating an employee or broadcasting their errant actions or thoughts? This will only be effective in lowering morale and encourage the employee to leave. Simply because you are knowledgeable doesn't mean all knowledge should be public! The ability to respect confidentiality and honor a confidence between subordinates, superiors, suppliers, customers and co-workers creates a trust that builds relationships within business. The inability to do the same quickly kills business relationships (and other relationships). Once again, this may appear to be common sense. But what did we say, there is no such thing as common sense.

Do you expand overseas?

In business and industry, many consider expansion into foreign countries. After all, we are a global market now, including both supply and demand. At what point do we consider sourcing from foreign countries or perhaps consider moving manufacturing overseas? Almost exclusively, the manufacturers for which I have worked have been international companies. Either we have imported or exported raw materials, components and finished goods – and sometimes both. What considerations should be taken into account when considering the global market? I can elude to some disasters and some successes. These are consistent with other companies I have audited. When working with an automotive supplier, our company considered eliminating the purchase of formed steel plates domestically. As an alternate, China was considered based upon much lower pricing. Full container quantities would need to be purchased based upon the freight costs and lead time for obtaining these plates. It did not make financial sense to purchase less than full container quantities. This also meant we would have 3-4 weeks of material on-hand upon delivery of each container. The lead time for ordering material was increased drastically, due to the production lead time of the Chinese facility, 6 week ocean delivery to the U.S., in addition to the subsequent travel from the port to our manufacturing plant. Price of material was substantially lower than our domestic suppliers as was labor costs in China, which meant our domestic supplier could not be competitive. Orders were placed with the Chinese supplier and orders were decreased domestically to allow for the reduction of domestic inventory during the 8 week period until Chinese material arrived. Finally the ocean container arrived at our plant. Shiny new plates were unloaded from the container, clearly marked with each part number, carefully packaged and at first appearance looked to be excellent quality. However looks can be deceiving. The plates which required a perfectly flat surface were skewed from side to side and front to rear. The holes drilled in the plates were incorrect size as well as located incorrectly on the plates. Forming was not to specifications and almost every measurable dimension was out of tolerance. Yes at this point the panic ensued! We had reduced our domestic inventory to the point where we could not run production. I'm sure you are asking the obvious question "Why didn't you obtain samples first?". Our company did obtain initial samples which were perfect in every dimension and quality was outstanding. These full production quantities were far from the quality of the samples however. Keep in mind, with a quality issue and 8 week lead time – replacement product was not readily available. Obviously our only option was to reorder from our domestic supplier, or shut down production for a period of time. Anybody in automotive manufacturing knows there was only one option. You can't shut down production! This by no means insinuates that all foreign suppliers are deficient in quality, nor would all suppliers not match their production runs to the same quality of sample materials. The lesson learned is that without easy access to review the manufacturing operation, their quality history, sample parts, work procedures and instructions, their quality standards and references from other customers – it prohibits purchasing/procurement from making an informed decision. Also, you know what other aspect of business you need to consider when evaluating the decision to import materials or products – the governmental legislation that exists along with pending legislation. While I am not aware of any legislation that would place such a high tariff on foreign companies which export to the U.S.A. that it makes more fiscal sense for them to produce in America, there are other areas that present tax and duty implications along with restricted materials, etc.... To fail to educate

yourself to these regulations could create a failure in your business. There

are also others that believe it is unethical to support foreign companies

if the option is available to support domestic companies. For most the

bottom line is the financial implications of importing. Just be certain that

importing does not create quality issues, freight issues and fee issues that

negate the benefit of the piece price. There are efforts to create

legislation that would focus on domestic manufacturing production, to

prevent the loss of American manufacturing and subsequently American

jobs. One suggestion is to tax foreign countries at such a high tariff level

that it is not fiscally responsible to export to the U.S. This will persuade

these companies to produce their goods in the U.S. It will also prevent

American companies from leaving the U.S. and moving to foreign

countries. It does strike me as curious that Toyota, Honda, Nissan, BMW,

Mercedes, Volkswagen, Kia, Hyundai, etc... find that it makes more

financial sense for them to build their vehicles in America for the

American market, when other formerly domestic automobile

manufacturers believe it is cheaper to build cars outside of the USA – and

subsequently sell these vehicles in the USA?! These foreign auto companies even persuaded many of their suppliers to move to America or have decided to source domestically – while the "former" Big 3 have chosen to import many of their component parts. Sure there are implications of unions in these decisions, but I will not be discussing the necessity or validity of unions in this book. That would justify an entire book in itself. In the end, businesses and industries must make the decisions that provide for a profitable environment and an environment in which to grow their business. Recently at a conference, a leader with an Asian-based toilet manufacturer eluded to the fact that their company could produce their products cheaper in the United States, than their facilities in China and India. He continued to express that although a cheaper labor force is present in these foreign countries; the cost of acquiring and importing materials and components, the efforts to find skilled workers, obtaining technology and the costs of exporting their finished goods proved much more costly than simply producing their product at the destination of their consumer market. Many manufacturers also "lost" their proprietary technology in foreign countries, thereby losing market share by new manufacturers that evolved in these countries. This appears to be a trend recognized by numerous manufacturers that are returning to the United States. Many were drawn by the extremely low labor costs 10-15 years ago. Even during the first 1-2 years of production in these foreign countries however, these companies began to recognize the mistake of locating to these countries.

Unfortunately such substantial capital investments had occurred, it was not an option to simply withdraw from these foreign investments. After all, a return of these investments had to be recognized before even considering moving back to the United States. However, there appears to be surge of companies moving back to the United States. But to further incentivize industry to return to the United States, additional changes need to occur. "We need to change our trade, tax and regulatory policies to help U. S. manufacturers be more competitive in both their home market and the global marketplace."[9] Just be certain you are aware of all factors that could affect your profitability and growth, before making such an important decision.

Summary

Whether manufacturing presents itself on a personal level or continues on a larger scale, success depends on adhering to the basic rules of business. Sales must exceed expenses. To ensure your company is capable of generating a profit, you must be aware of your costs, your inventory and your target market. If your creative or innovative idea has no demand, you will not be successful in growing a business. Accept the opinions and ideas of others, particularly those that daily perform the jobs you need in your business. Caution yourself to be open to new ideas, but recognizing that all ideas are not the best solution. Educate yourself by exposure to other companies, facts and research related to your product and business. Recruit those technical skills that you need for success. Work with local technical high schools and colleges to form curriculum and assist their programs, to fill the pipeline for future generations of employees. Hold yourself accountable to the highest ethics and morals, setting the example for your management team and employees. Expose yourself to govern-mental legislation that affects your organization, connecting the dots to issues that can be tied to your sustainability and growth. Recognize the economy is   global, but equally recognize caution when considering global relationships at the supply or customer level. While technology, healthcare, education, service industries and government jobs are essential parts of our workforce, manufacturing will continue to drive economic growth and prosperity. Manufacturing jobs are in demand along with the necessary technical skills sought after by industry. It is incumbent upon our society to spread this message to our younger generation. Elementary and middle school children need to be informed of the demand for these technical skills and the stability of retaining jobs in manufacturing, since most students are required to select an education path by high school. As parents, educators and businesses – let's train our kids in the basic survival skills to succeed in this world. I leave you with this quote:

"The objective of education is to prepare the young to educate themselves throughout their lives." Robert Maynard Hutchins

NOTES

1 – Discover Magazine : By David Kirby|Friday, March 18, 2011
2 - V. Ramanathan & G. Carmichael, supra note 1, at 226
3 - V. Ramanathan & G. Carmichael, supra note 1, at 226
4 – eetd.lbl.gov
5 - UNEP/GRID-Arendal, 'Black Carbon Emissions', UNEP/GRID-Arendal Maps
6 - Bouzereau, Laurent (1995). A Look Inside Jaws ["The Shark Is Not Working"]. Jaws: 30th Anniversary Edition DVD (2005): Universal Home Video
7 - Goldratt, Eliyahu M.; Jeff Cox. The Goal: A Process of Ongoing Improvement. Great Barrington, MA.: North River Press. ISBN 0-88427-061-0.
8 - Covey, Stephen R.; The 7 Habits of Highly Effective People, Free Press
9- Industry Week: Mar. 14, 2013, Michele Nash-Hoff, president, ElectroFab Sales